WHY I AM A CATHOLIC

Why I am a Catholic

Rowanne Pasco

Hodder & Stoughton
LONDON SYDNEY AUCKLAND

First published in Great Britain in 1995

10 9 8 7 6 5 4 3 2

British Library Cataloguing in Publication Data

A record for this book is available from the British Library

ISBN 0 340 63041 8

Typeset by Palimpsest Book Production Limited,
Polmont, Stirlingshire
Printed and bound in Great Britain by
Cox & Wyman, Reading, Berkshire

Hodder and Stoughton
A Division of Hodder Headline PLC
338 Euston Road
London NW1 3BH

Contents

Preface

Producing this book has given me quite a surprise. The list of people I set out to talk to about their Catholic faith was so varied that I expected a very varied response to the main question I was asking; 'Why are you a Catholic?' Although, as you will see from the following pages, the people included have different approaches to their faith, almost all of them are, to quote John Wilkins, 'happy to be a Catholic' and would not wish to be anything else.

Again and again I was impressed by the positive response which I got. Of course there were criticisms of the Catholic Church, even from Cardinal Hume, but, above all, each person showed a great love and respect for their Church, seeing it as the present-day representation of the community founded on Jesus Christ.

My own faith was certainly enlivened by each conversation I had, and I am grateful to everyone who agreed so generously to help, and who spoke to me so openly.

One of the reasons for the publication of this book is that 1995 marks the Centenary of Westminster Cathedral, the first Roman Catholic cathedral to be built in England since the Reformation. It is also a celebration of the complete return of the Catholic community into the full life of this country since those days. As the Catholic Church grows in stature and attracts ever more headlines and converts it is amazing to recall that until the nineteenth-century Catholics were suspect and downtrodden. They were not even allowed to stand for Parliament.

Things have changed. Catholics rejoice to have come out of the ghetto. Much of what has happened in England in recent years is due to the inspired and gentle leadership of Cardinal Basil Hume, to whom many of my contributors pay unsolicited credit.

My own answer to the question 'Why am I a Catholic?' is simply to quote the man put in charge of the community founded by Jesus, the Apostle Peter; 'Lord, to whom shall we go . . .?' The Barque of Peter may, as Clifford Longley says, be a 'rusty old ship', but after two thousand years of service it is still afloat. It continues to encounter stormy seas but shows no sign of sinking.

On a more practical level, I also owe my faith to the example of a great number of people who constantly show their love of the Lord in action. First I must thank my parents, especially my mother whose faith remains unshaken inspite of a great many trials. Then there are the many kind and generous Catholics I met during my ten years as editor of the *Universe* who did so much to help both my personal growth in faith and the growth of the paper. Finally I would like to thank my husband William who does so much to encourage my work and my faith.

Rowanne Pasco
Easter, 1995.

Cardinal Hume

Archbishop of Westminster

I started off life as a Catholic because my mother was a devout Catholic. But all of us, not only those who go to religious life or become priests, have to make our faith our own. There's an adult faith and a child's faith. The child's faith is what you receive from your parents, but then you have to make it your own and for most people that takes time. For me that was very much bound up with my becoming a monk. When I look back I realise just how young I was when I did that at 18. My early years in the monastery were not easy but I learned some very important truths, not only about myself, but about monastic life and about the Church. I've often said to people you join religious life for one reason but you remain in it for another, and you have to spend quite a number of years discovering what that reason is. You realise that what you have done is respond to an invitation even though it may have been in a rather muddled way. Certainly, when I found life difficult, the thing that kept me going was that I just had this deep conviction which was reinforced by some superiors, that this was what God wanted me to do. In a sense it didn't matter what I felt. That is when you really become adult in religious life when you know you've responded to a call and that you're prepared to follow Christ in that way of life whatever happens to you.

My mother's prayers also played a large part. I'm sure she prayed for a priest. Originally I was destined for the Dominicans. My decision was greatly influenced by meeting a wonderful Dominican, and I wanted to be like him. I was accepted by the Provincial when I was sixteen to go at a later date. But as I got older I got to know the Benedictines and suddenly realised this was where I ought to be and that's the way it was.

The monks at the monastery I joined worked in schools and parishes and I was attracted to this. I always said I wouldn't join a monastery that hadn't got parish work. When I was 18 or 19 in Newcastle we were just emerging out of the thirties and there was terrible poverty and the hardship I saw had a profound effect on me and made me want to do something to help, to minister to people as Christ ministered. I thought of it in a kind of crude and boyish way. But it played a big part in my decision to be a priest and to go into some sort of order.

When I was young I wanted to work as a priest and monk out in the world, in the market place, but as I got older I yearned for the desert, and I'd love to be able to retire into the desert now if I could. But I think I'd be happier doing that knowing that I've spent myself serving the Lord in the market place. I always said that a monk is authentically in the market place when really he'd prefer to be in the desert and had that yearning to be alone with the Lord and to be searching for God through meditation and prayer, though being an archbishop is certainly more interesting than being an abbot. I remember seeing my predecessor at Ampleforth going up the stairs one day and saying to myself, 'There goes the poor old abbot, too much to think about and not enough to do.' But here I've got too much to do and not enough time to think. I also wish I had more time to pray. I do miss choir office, for example. I had a marvellous experience a few years ago: I was fifty years a monk so I crept back to the monastery for a private retreat and quietly went to the Chapel of Saint Benedict and renewed my commitment to monastic life. I came away knowing I had been right those fifty years ago. That was where I belonged. It was a rare grace from the Lord to say, 'Yes, I did call you and you were right.' Of course I have experienced some doubts – we all have to go through that because for faith to grow it must be purified. That is very painful. But it is a rule of spirituality and that's when actually you commit yourself and when the really deep convictions emerge – that there is a God and that he's called you. After that the wobbles are not significant.

During these long years as a bishop one of the great experiences has been to see the unfolding of the Second Vatican Council. Now that I'm possibly near to the end of my job here I realise that there is still a long way to go for us to understand what the Holy Spirit was prompting at that Council. Even this last week I realised something that I hadn't realised before about the Council. It's very simple, and it is the centrality of the word of God. One pays lip service to that, but I think one of the very remarkable things in the Church at the moment is the number of people getting into groups to read and discuss the gospels. No one told them to do it, it's just happening. I should like to see far more of this because there is a great need for people to learn more about their faith.

The new Catechism is extremely important here. It is a great triumph. Some Catholic intellectuals criticised it because it doesn't always go in the direction that they would like it to, but the Catechism has to be a summary of where we are up to a certain point. Theologians are right to go forward and explore, but the main bulk of the people need something very traditional, certain, tried and clear.

I have to remain in the Church because I know that the guidance and the teaching I get is prompted by the Holy

Spirit. It is a special guidance promised to the Holy Father, and to the College of Bishops in communion with him. So I have no problem when pronouncements come from Rome which are genuinely from the Holy Father. If I find them difficult or don't understand them I realise it is because my human mind is too small. I like that guarantee of the guidance of the Holy Spirit.

But of course there are distinctions to be made between various pronouncements. There are solemn ones and less solemn ones. It's highly technical how you interpret that but I know if the Holy Father goes on plugging a line then the Holy Spirit is with him. It is certainly more likely to be with him than anybody else. Although some things are done in his name or by the Curia, which I wouldn't necessarily agree with. I would like to see an improvement in consultation in the Church. This is extremely difficult because it's only worth consulting people who know what they are talking about. When some documents come from Rome I do feel there hasn't been sufficient consultation. Although there is often more than people think. I've always been convinced of the fragility of the people who run the Church. It would have been much more sensible if God had brought angels down to do it properly. But He didn't. It is a human organisation handling very sacred things and it is bound to go wrong from time to time.

I do find it difficult to see how the Pope is sometimes condemned for being authoritarian. What people don't like is what he says about abortion, contraception, divorce and sexual mores in general. He is very hard on all these things but at the same time, I would urge people to read his book, *On the Threshold of Hope.* You will see that he is absolutely consistent all the way, trying to get across the basic idea of the beauty and majesty of humanity. He criticises capitalism because it overemphasises the individual and neglects the neighbour – the community – and he is against collectivism and Marxism because they concentrate on the collective at the cost of the individual. The vision of the dignity of the human person has dominated the whole of his pontificate. So he sees things like contraception, abortion and euthanasia as a total contradiction. Also, he has a profound feeling about the importance of the family and marriage. The Church must do more to help in both these areas. I had to wait four years before I was allowed to make my vows as a monk. That commitment only involved me, yet we let people cheerfully go into marriage with little preparation and often they are very immature. Society must say, 'Marriage is extremely important. You may not get married until you are properly prepared, for the sake of yourselves and everybody else.' Parishes should help more, but it can't all be done by the priest. Lay people, especially married couples, must do what they can too.

Divorce and separation cause me great concern because I know how those involved suffer. I am also concerned about the homosexual community, laicised priests, the homeless, the jobless, especially the young unemployed, the loveless and those who suffer cruelty throughout the world. I adhere totally to the Church's teaching on sexual morality, but I do have compassion for those in difficult situations who are in agony and I wish more could be done for them. I just say stay with us because we shall always try to do what we can for you. Don't walk away. I know that many do go – they stop coming to the Church. All I would say to them is what the Lord said to some of the Apostles, 'Come and see, come and see.' Often what they come to see is whether a church service is going to touch or move them. If it does not, that is sad.

Something I say quite a lot in talks is that our society is opaque as far as the things of God are concerned. But then look in the heart of every man, woman and child and you see an emptiness that is waiting to be filled. The Church's task now, for priests, the laity, everybody, is to say, 'How do we help to fill that empty space?' The only way, I believe, is telling people about our Lord and his great love. We must help them to see that God is the centre. That's what matters. If you take yourself very seriously maybe you haven't got enough trust in God. I now increasingly pray that marvellous prayer of our Lord, 'Into Thy hands, Lord, I commend my spirit'. He said it on the cross straight after, 'My God, my God, why has thou forsaken me?' In both cases the prayer comes from a psalm. It doesn't matter what problems you're dealing with and what darkness you experience and what ghastly things happen to you. Sometimes one feels one has been forsaken; yet 'into Thy hands' is a marvellous prayer and is a whole attitude towards God of trust and confidence. You see, it doesn't all depend on you. When I say that prayer I do experience peace, but I'm not good at it – I'm still practising. I can't yet have that trust and confidence in God which I know I should.

Fr Graham Leonard

Retired Anglican Bishop, now a Catholic priest

It was much more than the ordination of women that made me decide to become a Roman Catholic. I had already been very concerned because I had come to see that the basic teaching documents of the Church of England, the Anglican formularies as they are known – including the Book of Common Prayer, with the thirty-nine Articles – were being interpreted in different ways by Evangelicals, Protestants and liberal Anglicans. It seemed to me that instead of living under the judgement of Revelation, we were in fact trying to decide what that should be to suit our times. I was also concerned that the governing body of the Church of England – the Synod – could do exactly as it liked, ignoring the vast majority of Christendom. In a sense, the ordination of women, which I believe raise profound theological issues, was the trigger that finally made me say, 'I can't go on teaching in the name of the Church of England, or the Anglican Church.'

For all those years I genuinely believed it was possible to live a Catholic life in the Church of England. Then I came to realise that the Catholic interpretation which I was trying to give, and believed could be given, to Anglicanism, in fact all came from the Roman Catholic Church. The other thing that attracted me so much about the Roman Catholic Church was its sense of the awe and mystery of God which draws you to Him although you do not wholly understand it. I had always felt the Roman Catholic Church stood for a supernatural religion in a way which the Church of England did not. Another point, of course, was the fact that Roman Catholic doctrine was declared by the Magisterium of the Church. When I go anywhere to preach or teach, I do not have to explain, 'This is what the Faith is' as I often had to in the Church of England. Now I can say, given what the Church teaches, how do we, in fact, implement that? How do we live it? This has brought a great sense of freedom and serenity. I no longer feel I am subject to whatever the latest scholar happens to be saying.

Becoming a Catholic has also helped me develop my relationship with God. I have always said my prayers, the Office and so on, but they mean something very different now. I want to pray in a way that I didn't before. For example, when I wake up in the middle of the night, instead of worrying about things, I simply pray. Now it is not something I just do because it's what I am told to do, but because I want to pray, to talk to God, to hear Him and to love Him. This has been one of the greatest changes. I am very lucky to be allowed my own little oratory at my home where I can also say Mass and my wife is the congregation. She became a Catholic a few weeks after I did. I reckon I spend at least half an hour every day just in contemplation. In a way one prays all the time.

For many years when I was Bishop of London, I told people in my sermons that the one thing that matters above all else is your relationship with God, because when you die that is all you're going to have to take with you. I could see this in all sorts of ways, but that has become luminously clear to me since I became a Roman Catholic, and in a very fresh and living way. It is something which has appeared, not as a result of what I've done, but it is something that God has given me, which is marvellous.

I also feel more relaxed since I became a Catholic, because I don't feel it all depends on me. I'm not forever having to go out and fight battles and make statements about where I stand and this kind of thing. It is much more a question of listening to what God says, seeing what that means and being able to live in a relationship of loving obedience to Him. I mentioned the word obedience and that seems to me absolutely fundamental because the whole of the scriptures speak to me of sacrificial obedience, which one very seldom hears anything about nowadays in the Church of England. I'm sorry to have to criticise, but I think that's true. Whereas I find now that obedience is taken for granted. People may rebel against it, they may not like it, but obedience in love is an integral part of the Christian life. I have been to a variety of places since I became a Catholic and met all kinds of people, and I have found this sense of living under obedience in love is fundamental.

I find it difficult to understand why some people who want to call themselves Catholic don't want to accept the Magisterium and I am surprised that some Catholics are critical of the Pope, although I don't find much of that among what I would call members of ordinary congregations.

The Church's emphasis on authority and obedience is not a restriction on my freedom – I was originally trained as a scientist – if I was going to be free to do research, it meant accepting certain observed characteristics about the matter of things I was examining. These bound me and I could not pretend that this material, or that substance, was not what it was. Only when I accepted the characteristics of that substance was I actually free to use it, experiment with it and develop on beyond it. So for me, accepting the basic truths of the faith sets me free in a similar way, free to explore their significance and their meaning and to see how far they reflect on the one hand our imperfections and, on the other, what is eternal and what is transcendent.

One of the major differences between the Catholic Church and other Christian denominations is that there is a continuity between the early Church and the present Catholic Church, which doesn't exist with the others. Whether you take the Protestant Church on the continent, or the Church of England here, they have sort of bypassed the Middle Ages and tried to go back to the primitive Church. So where is the continuity of the faith? Newman wrote, 'Did Saint Athanasius or Saint Ambrose come suddenly to life, it cannot be doubted what communion he would take to be his own.' The Catholic Church certainly does have this continuity right back to the earliest days and, indeed, to the Lord himself.

Then, as I see it, the Catholic Church does try to live under the judgment of the original revelation. I know it has developed this, but it has not at any point deviated from it or been wholly dominated by a particular time in history or particular trend in human thought. There have been great movements, for example, at one time scholasticism was predominant in Catholic thought, but it is not a universal characteristic which has gone right through time. Just as there have been great figures in the Catholic Church, like Saint Augustine, or Thomas Aquinas, they have not been sources of theological division in the way that, say, Luther or Calvin were. Another important aspect of the Catholic Church is the fact that it sees itself as existing for everybody and has never been an exclusive sect. It has opened its doors and said, 'We welcome everybody. Here's the way for repentance, forgiveness, for union with God in Christ.' It is not for the elect but for sinners.

One of the wonderful things about the Roman Catholic Church are the sacraments and the fact that I can partake of them, not because I am righteous, but because of God's great mercy. A particular phrase in the Book of Common Prayer had an enormous influence on me: 'We do not presume to come to this table, O Lord, trusting in our own righteousness but in thy manifold and great mercies.' Although I am sinful, I can come to the sacraments, trusting in God's promises and power. Not relying on what I am.

A great difference between myself and other Catholic priests is, of course, that I am married and have been for fifty-two years, but I am not in favour of married clergy being the norm in our secular society. Marriage for clergy places enormous stress in two ways; first, a man and a woman are not necessarily at the same point in their Christian discipleship and, even if they are, they will not necessarily remain there. This is especially difficult if the man is a priest. The other thing is that being a priest can put a strain on family life. I know this from children of clergy families who can find it sometimes very difficult in a secular society where their father's occupation is the subject of criticism or scorn.

Then there is the problem of where the priest is serving. It may be in his best interest to move, but perhaps he cannot take his children away from the local school. And I do not believe that sexual relationships are absolutely essential for living a full human life. Plenty of friends of ours who are not married, are extremely fulfilled people, often even saintly. They are not in any way lacking because they are not married. Our Lord lived a totally full human life as a single man.

As I said, the ordination of women was the trigger that made me decide to leave the Church of England – and I would find it difficult if the Roman Catholic Church did the same, although I do not believe it will happen. Men and women are equal, but they are also complementary. I don't believe it was an accident that at the Incarnation God became a male human being though, of course, God is beyond gender. And if, as some people say, something cannot be fully representative of humanity unless it's done by both men and women, well, what is the implication of that for the Incarnation? Really, the logical development is that you need another Incarnation, God being born as a woman. Ordaining women as priests doesn't really help.

I also believe that there are profound differences between men and women. My wife has a better degree than I have, for example. She is very intelligent, but we think differently. We differ because I am a man and she is a woman and I believe that to try and blur this distinction is alarming.

It's extraordinary to think that when I was a boy, Rome seemed like a different planet. To become a Catholic was almost like changing your nationality. Yet now there is nothing that I find especially difficult about belonging to the Catholic Church. There are small things occasionally like having to sing little ditties which pass for hymns, and I have never greatly loved hymns. Also the desire for everyone to do something leads to a kind of mateyness and lack of reverence that I find hard to take. On the other hand, I think that the simplicity and directness of the modern Mass is wonderful. One regret I have is that the Mass no longer ends with the opening of Saint John's gospel, which has always been my favourite scripture reading. Saint John seems to have the most wonderful blend of grasping the reality of the Incarnation, coupled with an extraordinary emphasis on love, and this is so well expressed in this reading.

Overall, since I became Catholic, I have experienced an extraordinary sense of joy and freedom. I don't think that's just because I've retired. After all, I retired in May 1991 and was not received into the Catholic Church until April 1994. I do not miss being a bishop – I can do all that is important to me as a priest, say Mass, hear confessions, preach and minister to the sick. That is more than enough for any man, and I am being kept very busy.

Sister Wendy Beckett

Carmelite nun and TV presenter on art

I am a Catholic first and foremost because I had the good fortune to be born into a Catholic family. But that is, of course, not the only reason. I suspect that many people think that to have been born and educated as a Catholic means that one *is* a Catholic, but this is not so. The image I would use is a child who at birth may be given a gift of membership of a tennis club, That is very nice but it is obviously meaningless unless the child grows up to have an interest in tennis, goes to the club, uses the facilities and learns what it is all about. Many people do not have the good fortune to have someone explain to them what the faith is all about. When you do understand it, it is as plain as two and two make four. It is the complete answer to all the longings of the human heart and it is a means to an end. The end is Our Blessed Lord, and the faith takes you there with directness. But you have to have the good fortune to understand it.

From my earliest years it was obvious to me that the faith was important. I learned this from my parents who were the sweetest, warmest people. God was important to them. It would have been inconceivable to them to miss Mass, for instance.

Somehow I knew within myself, when I was about four, that God was everything, our complete happiness. I started school at that time and I must have been a very naughty child. I went to the Sacred Heart Convent school in Edinburgh when I was small, and I remember two things clearly; one day, coming home from school, I was enraptured with the knowledge of how never to be naughty again. Sister had told us that if we were tempted to be naughty, all we had to do was to say the Holy Name of Jesus and all the desire to be naughty would disappear. I felt the Great Key to happiness had been put into my hand. I remember vividly that journey home from school, knowing that I had that Key. And, it always has worked. It is perfectly true, if ever you want to do anything unworthy of your humanity, simply say the name Jesus, let Our Lord into your heart and you will not want to hurt Him. But I suppose, even at that young age, this advice might not have meant much if Jesus had not already been very important to me.

My second memory is of when I made my first Holy Communion. Sister told us that, on that day, Jesus would speak to us in our hearts. I couldn't wait. I remember, plain, lumpy child that I was, coming back from the Communion rails in my white satin dress and veil, and kneeling down and closing my eyes and waiting for him to speak to me. I waited and waited, and then, suddenly, it dawned on me; that's how He speaks. He speaks in silence, not words. He speaks in waiting. That was a very happy insight. I just understood that to be waiting, to be listening, was to be hearing Him. If you listen, in the nothingness and the silence, God speaks to you. This is a very mature approach for a child, so I count myself very lucky. That realisation made everything I had been taught live for me.

I had been with three different communities of nuns; the Sacred Heart, the Dominicans, the German Dominicans, and the Notre Dame sisters. Guilt was never any part of their teaching. Even confession is not really about sin or guilt.

If you ever hurt God and then say you are sorry, can you imagine Him *not* saying, 'That's all right, Love'? Confession or reconciliation as we now call it, is about putting right the damage we have done to the world by not loving Him enough. I go to confession every week with great joy. I also came to see that God was, above all, complete forgiveness and joy. When we do wrong we should feel sorrow; not guilt. Everyone goes wrong sometimes, and all God asks is for you to let Him come to you through the Church and the sacraments. Confession is like plugging into electricity. You let Our Blessed Lord accept your sorrow for lack of love. It is a most joyful sacrament and I don't think we should degrade it with a long list of all the petty things that God has forgiven already.

Sacraments are vital. We are body and soul and the sacraments are the way our bodies become instruments of receiving God's love. I cannot imagine anybody not wanting to go to Mass every day, I couldn't live without it. When I was making my programmes for the BBC, I said that I would do absolutely anything for them as long as they got me to daily Mass. At Mass we are taken out of our poor little selves with our lack of love, into the enormous, redemptive love of Our Blessed Lord. Too many people think they can bypass Jesus and get directly to God, but they can't. Jesus said; 'No one can come to the Father except through me. I am the way.' That's it, you see, God is complete mystery. Only one person, Jesus, has seen Him, and He tells us, 'God is Father' and we can't reach Him on our own.'

I cannot remember when I decided to become a nun. It seems it was always in my mind because I felt it was the only way to love God completely. Certainly, it was not because I was a good child. I remember my mother saying, one day; 'Oh, Wendy, one day you will be a nun and people will think you are holy, and only I will know how difficult you are.' That's true. I was a deeply selfish person and I still am.

That is why I, and all of us, need the Mass. Every time we go to Mass we let Our Blessed Lord take us out of our smallness into His greatness. Some of those onion-layers of selfishness get peeled off. I am very hopeful for myself. I expect to be able really to love Him by the time it all ends, but as I said I couldn't do it without the Mass and the sacraments.

With regard to vocations, nowadays a girl of sixteen would not be allowed to become a nun. We would say: 'You are too young. You must get your education, have boyfriends, know about money.' But, when I was sixteen it was right for me. Perhaps it was because I was inadequate; I don't have room in my life for deep, intimate friendships with anybody. But it has all worked out very happily. More than that, it has surpassed my wildest dreams. That does not mean that I am always totally happy. It is a hard life, and sometimes painful. So many God-given desires have to be denied. But I was lucky. I didn't have desires for a family and all that.

Of course, you can be a nun without being a Catholic. There are Anglican nuns, and they are so close to us that I hate making distinctions, but the only way I could be a nun, shabby nun that I am, was by being a Catholic because, as I said, I need the sacraments.

The lack of priests is terrible (and I am totally against Communion Services; they are not the Mass). Why are we short of priests when there are all those married men, and, indeed women, who are just dying to be ordained? So many people would make wonderful priests but they are barred because of official rules. The Holy Spirit is speaking to the Church through this situation but the Church has not yet heard. Yet the Church is not just the hierarchy. It is all of us, and we are voting with our feet. The Church should be wise, glorious, leading us nobly into the future. But it is not; it is a poor, wounded Church, stumbling forward, making mistakes because it is made up of human beings. That is the real Church; the

Church of Jesus; the Church that moves at the pace of the slowest.

Galileo said that the earth moved round the sun, and not vice versa, over five hundred years ago. But the Vatican only recently apologised for the Church's treatment of him, even though the rest of the world had long accepted his ideas. This is how the Church works; it is painful. We must not expect it always to make the right decision, but we have to work, with complete loyalty and utter faith, that eventually the Church will hear what the Spirit is telling it. None of us is going to leave the Church just because it is slow to learn, or walk out just because it is wounded.

I don't think for a moment that we should be angels, having no dark emotions. If we look at the gospels we see that Our Lord himself was upset by things. For example, he agonised in the Garden of Olives before the crucifixion. Any idea that we should be able to walk, smiling, into the operating theatre is false.

I am convinced that the deepest thing in our faith is joy. It is deeper than sorrow. Every crucifixion ends in resurrection. This is not understood. If we linger on the crucifixion we are missing the fact that it is all made into joy.

In 1970, I made a film with the BBC about the windows in King's College, Cambridge, and when we came to the crucifixion, it dawned on me that Jesus died in a blaze of joy. He said, 'I have done it.' He was the only human being who had ever absolutely achieved all that God asked of him, so he must have died in absolute ecstasy of happiness and gratitude. Ever since that realisation I can never think of his suffering without remembering the joy that he had from knowing that he had given his Father all, trusting Him to redeem all, even those who did not know Him. Our faith always points us to what I call 'Jesus joy'. This is not the same as human joy; it does not mean that things will be made easy for you. What it does mean is that, whatever happens, God will be with you to make it fruitful. Prayer may not save me from a plane crash, but it does mean that if I do crash, God will enter that crash with me and make it redemptive.

I have met very few people who understood what it truly means to be a Catholic. Even some who are very devout do not understand that they have been completely liberated by the binding of God's love.

Even when it seems that some rules in the Church are unintelligent and should change, still, in keeping them and accepting all the burdens of love, we are setting ourselves free. Mind you, I do not think that all Church rules are right, for example in sexual matters. This is understandable, for the world has not really got it right and we cannot expect the Church to be ahead of its time. It is hard to get the balance between the burden that you need and the burden that is excessive.

I began writing about art to earn money for my community. Somebody who read what I wrote thought I might be good talking about it and asked me to make a film for television. Since I had never seen television I was quite happy to try. Then, somebody else saw that film and it grew . . . If, six years ago, anyone had said to me, 'Would you be willing to leave your caravan in Norfolk and come to London?' I should have replied, 'Absolutely not'. But God works otherwise. You take one step, and then another and another. He leads you. If I didn't think my work in art was good, I would not do it. It is not what I would have chosen.

All this public exposure on television and in print has been a totally purifying experience. Working with the BBC has shown me for the first time how angry I can be. Filming can be very frustrating. I had felt I was placid. It has also shown me how selfish I can be and how great is my need of God. As I wrote recently, my love of art is for me a way of loving God. Art is essentially beauty that draws us into the truth of our own being, and whenever we have truth and beauty, we have God. And I think I am getting to the end of it now, physically. I always believed that God would tell me when He had enough.

Fr Michael Hollings

Parish priest and author of many books on prayer

My father wasn't a Catholic but my mother was a very strong one. In a peculiar way, through her I am descended directly from a cardinal of the Holy Roman Church. Cardinal Weld as a layman was married. When his wife died, leaving him with one daughter, he became a priest, then a cardinal and she married, so his family continued through her.

Mother brought all three of us children up as Catholics and we all maintained the faith. But I had a period during my wartime service when I sort of lapsed, partly through laziness and partly through disillusion with war. It was so terrible with all around you dying. As a young soldier I was terrified, but that did not turn me to God. The only good thing about the war was the personal relationships which developed between comrades, they were so important. We were living merely to live, so we had mad drinks parties and things like that. During that time I didn't really believe in anything. Then I was wounded. I was not particularly interested in whether I was dying or not. I just felt terribly fed up and ill. But I pulled through.

I came back to my faith at the end of the Second World War. A series of things made me think again. One was that my mother said that she was dying of cancer and would I come home. It was just at a time when I was available to go home because I had been out in Italy longer than any of my counterparts. But one of them came to me and said, 'Michael, I'm 43, with a family in England. May I go home instead of you?' I was only 23 and had this awful choice, whether to go home to my mother or to let him go. I had to pray about it, even though I didn't believe much. So I prayed and I let him go to his family. Having to make this awful decision brought me back to prayer and to the Faith. After that I again asked to go home. I was refused and told that the only way to get back home was by volunteering to go to Palestine. So I did that and when I got back to England I said that my mother was dying, could I go to her. They said, no, you have got to go to Palestine. Just as I got there, my mother died and I asked again to go home and they said no. I was full of angst and thoroughly fed up with being in the army, Suddenly I felt I was hit by God. I had, as it were, been reclaimed by Him and his love and I came back to belief and to prayer. I couldn't say I had missed being away from the Faith, but when I came back there was a real sense of joy and purpose.

So I went around to the chaplain and said, 'I want to be a priest, I want to help people.' It was a huge jump, but I am like that; in for a penny – in for a pound. He looked at me and said: 'But you don't even go to church, why don't you become a social worker?' And I said, 'I don't want to.' That was in 1945. Then I tried to get out of the army and wrote to Cardinal Griffin at Westminster. I also had a very good friend in Monsignor Vernon Johnson, an Anglican who had become a Catholic, who also put in a word for me with the Cardinal. By the time I got home, Cardinal Griffin had arranged for me to go to the Beda College, a seminary for mature students in Rome. I was then 24. So I went and saw Cardinal Griffin, in my uniform and he said, 'Now, Major Hollings, you are 34, aren't you?' And I said, 'I'm sorry, I am only 24.' His face fell somewhat, but nevertheless I was sent off to the Beda and was the youngest student there.

I found the college was absolute hell, and extremely cold. I couldn't understand philosophy, so every afternoon I used to go to the church in Piazza San Silvestro where there was perpetual adoration of the Blessed Sacrament. I just prayed there and sometimes even slept. I often used to go to the convent close to the Gregorian University which was run by the nuns from Wimbledon. They had Benediction at five in the afternoon. So, I spent each afternoon, from two till five-thirty, praying. Then I would come back to the college and get on with what study I could. I thought that I had gone there to help others, but apart from the students there was no one to help.

As so often happens with us clergy, we often tend to do all the work ourselves and so the terrible difficulty I found, and still find, is that no one is saying how much one depends on God. In fact, when one is going hell-for-leather to keep up the number of Masses or instructions or whatever, what you have to learn, and I learn it more and more as I grow older, is the extreme importance of letting go. Letting God do it instead of doing it yourself. There is a fine line between that and just sitting around all day, letting God look after everything.

I could not do my work without prayer and I find the Catholic Church's prayer-structure helps me enormously, especially the Mass and the Office. I like to get up early to pray. When I was a chaplain at Oxford the students used to come in and talk till two in the morning, so I couldn't get up terribly early. But nowadays I get up at half-past four. I make the sign of the cross as soon as I wake up. Then I dress quickly and I go into the church and stay there till about a quarter to six, some of the time in the dark, in prayer, some of it saying the Office. That time is just given to God completely. I find this immensely valuable. It sets the tone for the day. When

I come up I tackle the various chores, breakfast and things like that, then I go to the church again for Morning Prayer at seven-thirty and celebrate Mass at eight. After that it really depends on how the day goes, as to how much prayer I can actually fit in. Often during the day I use some type of mantra prayer where you make a little ejaculation as you walk along the street. And when anyone says; 'Pray for me' I say 'Right! We'll do it now' and do it in the street or wherever it may be. It brings them up short. Whenever a person comes, I try to say a prayer with them before they go. So, really there's a sense of praying all the time.

When I came into London I was appointed to Saint Patrick's, Soho, and I used to get up early and pray considerably, much to the distress of my senior curate, who though I was quite wrong to get up so early to pray. Then I was appointed to Westminster Cathedral. There we had all the Offices in choir, which I can't say I really enjoyed. It was extremely difficult in choir – all this 'turn left, turn right', you know. Anyway I can't sing, so it really was a trial and a burden doing the Office and I found that the best way to pray was to stand quietly at the back of the church (which 'wasn't done' at the Cathedral). There I found all sorts of different people, with so many different problems for whom I could pray. Nowadays I live in what we call an 'open parish' with all sorts of people coming and going all the time.

One of the difficulties in life is listening. But in prayer, you listen to God. Most of the time you are fairly blank or being distracted or whatever. God doesn't speak very loudly at times. Sometimes He doesn't speak at all. You just patiently listen, that is a wonderful foundation for learning to listen to other people. They gain a lot just being able to talk to somebody who is prepared to listen. You don't necessarily have to say anything, but at the end of the session they get up and say 'Thank you so much'. And you say, 'Well, thank God' and 'let's say a prayer'.

I think we are in a sad period now, where so many things are thrust at us from all directions, so many people claiming they can cure or heal people, supplying nostrums. And that's one of the reasons that the Sacrament of Confession seems to be less popular. I hear a lot of confessions up in my room rather than in a confession-box. It is easier to talk in the informal setting. Also, many have come to realise that you do get forgiveness at Mass any time you go, at least for ordinary peccadilloes. Absolution is given at the beginning of Mass and when you go to Holy Communion you put yourself before God. That's your normal way of asking and receiving forgiveness. Then, rather like going to the dentist, you occasionally come along to the priest for a deeper treatment. He may be able to see a problem, much as the dentist may spot the decay in your tooth although you can't feel anything yet. Formal confession is an opportunity for deeper conversion and some spiritual direction at the same time. I meet my confessor three or four times a year. And that, I think, is very sensible.

I have been enormously privileged to meet so many wonderful people who have helped me with my faith. I was very much influenced by Vernon Johnston, the man who had originally helped me to see the Cardinal. There's also a wonderful man in Rome, named Benedict Williamson, a convert too. He had been an architect and a priest in Southwark diocese and then he went to live with the Blue Sisters in Rome. He was my guide at the time. He was very old and very holy. One of his favourite phrases, when things were going totally wrong, was, 'This is a day made in Heaven'.

When I was in Rome, and much against my will at first, I was persuaded to go to see Padre Pio, the Franciscan friar who had the stigmata, the wounds of Christ on his body. Once I had been there, I went as often as I could. Sometimes, at Easter or Whitsun or whenever it might be, I would spend a few days near the monastery of San Giovanni Rotondo, where he lived and I got to know him very well. He took me on as one of his 'Spiritual Children'. He was so ordinary and simple and totally taken up in God. His Mass used to last an hour and a half. He didn't do anything spectacular but he went into total deep silence. Just to be there was the important thing. Then, when you met him outside, he would give you a friendly cuff on the head and promise to pray. In him the ordinary was extraordinary. But he also had a practical side; he founded a hospital, for example.

At a later stage, I got to know Mother Teresa when I asked her to come and start a convent in London. She stayed with us for a bit and then we found her a house and she founded the convent in Southall. I have been involved with her ever since. A very remarkable person. Every time she comes to Britain I see her and say Mass for her. It has been marvellous to meet all these extraordinary people, I have been so lucky.

I also have many close ecumenical contacts. and have very great respect and love for other Christians, especially the Anglicans and the Methodists and have done a lot of work with them. I had a long and very lovely association with the great Methodist Doctor Sangster. Soon after I came back from the Beda I used to go to see him in his house and we would talk about spiritual matters. It was he who told me that two great men, John Wesley and John Henry Newman, spent four hours a day in prayer. As far as I am concerned, the quicker we all get to intercommunion, the sharing of the Eucharist, the better. I am afraid a lot of other people don't go along with me on that.

I suppose the main reason I am a Catholic is that I was born one. Most people stay with the religion they were born into. If I had been born in Saudi Arabia I should probably have been a Muslim. Other people get the urge to change. However, for all the lovable things about the other churches, I still feel that the Catholic Church is *The Church.* I have a great loyalty to it and feel I have been totally blessed, both by being in it and by meeting all those people whom I have met through it. It does have its difficulties, but it has given me a wonderfully happy life.

One of the great things about the Church is the wonderful variety of people it touches. It used to be said that the Church of England was the Tory party at prayer, but that has not been so with the Catholic Church. There is a great sense of being the church of the ordinary people. That's a real joy. And it is not just the variety of classes, if you can use that word (in the good sense), but also the variety of races. In my early days, the Catholic Church was very much the church of the Irish, although there were exceptions, like the writers Chesterton and Belloc, who came in from a different background. Fortunately, I was appointed to Saint Patrick's in Soho, where you met a wonderful variety of people straight away, the prostitutes and so on. The priests were able to walk through the streets without any worry, while the police had to go in pairs.

With regard to the teachings of the Church, there is quite a lot you have to take on faith, but I don't find that difficult. Obviously some teachings are more important than others. For example, I don't set the Assumption very high.

One of the things the Church must tackle, however, is the position of women. I didn't always feel that, but I do now. One of my best friends was Etta Gullick, an Anglican who spent a lot of time preaching and giving retreats. We wrote several books together, including some on prayer. I feel, however, we have a long way to go before we get to women priests. Bishop B.C. Butler once said that he couldn't find anything in scripture or tradition against women priests, but still, he hoped it wouldn't happen while he was alive.

I think also that the Church must think again about the way that it treats homosexuals; its attitude can be very harsh towards them. These are people who have not voluntarily taken a vow of celibacy and they should be allowed to have a fulfilled life. The thing that I would try to bring home to them is the type of relationship. It should be stable. The problem is promiscuity.

One of my greatest wishes is to see lay people more involved in running the Church. In the past, they have not been encouraged to play their full part and too much of what they could have done was left to the priests. I have always been fascinated by the work of lay people in the Church, particularly the Young Christian Workers. They led me into real discussions and actions which were enormously constructive in my life, introducing me to unions and shop floors, hard living, confined family life, great aspirations and expectations; young men and women who had had none of the 'advantages' that I had had, but were solidly, happily, strongly faithful both to God and to the people. I wish I could feel I had given them anything comparable to what they gave me.

What of the Church since Vatican II? Well, the Council began something all right; a great shaking of the ground, opening of windows and letting in air and light. Not comfortable, but the Church was never intended to be comfortable, any more than the following of Christ is comfortable. Certainly, the Council caused frustration and uncertainty among some of the clergy, especially those who were set in their ways. Part of the problem of the modern Church, specially here in Britain, is that some people, young and old alike, are clinging to the past for fear of losing something. It takes courage to set out on the path set by Vatican II. Personally, I know I didn't realise what a great man Pope Paul VI, helmsman of the Council, was until after he was dead. You have only got to re-read some of his writings, as I did.

I think that for anyone who has lapsed from the Faith, there is always a way back. It may be very slow, or it may not, but they should never be afraid of trying.

Patricia Hayes

Actress, President of the Catholic Stage Guild

I'm a Catholic because I was born one. My mother was a very staunch Irish Catholic. The two things went together; you stood up for the Irish and you stood up for Catholics. We were brought up to do that as children. But my father was a very strong Protestant. He was Irish too, and belonged to what was called the Protestant Ascendancy. His parents were shattered because he was the only one of their children who married and he married a Catholic. But he was in all ways far the best person in our family, a wonderful man, so innately good and kind, long-suffering, enormously amusing and entertaining.

He was received into the Church on his death bed because he did not want to become a Catholic until his mother passed on. He felt it would be the most terrible grief to her to think that he had deserted what for her was the true religion. But I will say this for my grandparents, although they were deeply Protestant, they never took it out on us. Their maids would take us to Mass when we were in Cork on holiday and they were absolutely delighted that we were on their side, as it were.

My mother kept to the rule of not missing Mass on Sundays. She'd say, 'Come along, everybody out, it's Sunday.' She wasn't very religious, though she did believe in prayer, and she thought that if you kept the Commandments or if you led a good Catholic life you would die having no regrets. I am not really a devout Catholic, and I sometimes say to my son, who is a much better, more devoted Catholic than I am, 'The Mass is ruined by people all talking together, all saying the same prayer.' I suppose it's because I'm an actress that I want to be out in front telling them how to say it, all that awful mumbling, rattling it all off like that is meaningless to me. My son says we've got to give the people who are not good actors their chance to perform as well.

I don't often go to Mass now because I'm in my 80s, I'm not really fit to. On the whole I don't any longer think that if I don't go to Mass one week that it is a mortal sin. I am trying not to believe in mortal sin, though I might get a terrible shock when I die. I just feel that that you should do the best you can. But I do believe that rules and regulations are very good when you're young because they give you a standard to aim for.

Often if I go to the Catholic Stage Guild, which I belong to I like to read the actor's prayer, which is very beautiful:

Prayer for an Actor

My Jesus, bless me in this my actor's life. Whether I draw tears from the audience or make them laugh, off stage let me be serious minded, yet keep my sorrows behind the scenes. May I be undeceived by success and undismayed by failure. Make me generous towards the work of others and a good influence wherever I may go. Let me always return to the Sacraments, however often things go wrong.

On stage, off stage,
In life, in death,
Jesus have mercy
On my soul.

Because I'm a good reader everybody is spellbound, especially if they haven't heard it before. It's a gorgeous prayer. Recently I was visiting my daughter, who doesn't bother with religion really, although she leads a very good life, and she said, 'It's Palm Sunday, would you like me to get some neighbours to take you to Mass?' and I said I would. The woman who took me said I just want to have a quick word with Father before the Mass. She came out and said that he wanted to meet me. He said, 'I want you to read the whole of the gospel today,' and I asked, 'Who would read it if I weren't here?' and he replied, 'We spread it out amongst the congregation.' I agreed, but I had no time to look at it, it was just handed to me like that.

I'm always slightly ahead as I read just to keep the sense there, and I've got all my years of acting experience. So I read it and there was absolute silence right through. A few weeks later I met a woman in the village who said, 'After you read the gospel on Sunday, we women got together and said, if only it could be read to us like that every Sunday, the church would be packed.'

Many priests are not aware of things like that, but the women are. It's better to have no sermon at all than to have one given by a crashing bore. If you can't hold people's attention, you only get those who have nothing better to do.

It should be a pleasure to go to Mass. I'm sure in some countries it's more lively. If you get a good sermon everybody listens; you might think, 'Oh God, the sermon,' but once it gets going, if it's really interesting and challenging, you think, 'This is interesting.' Church is not meant to be boring, and the trouble with it is that it very often is.

In my early days in rep or on tour I always went to Mass because I was brought up to believe it was a mortal sin to miss it. After you had been there was always a feeling of being glad to have done it. It's possibly true that just going to Mass, being there, is a help because sometimes you are making a huge sacrifice by going when it doesn't suit you at all.

I don't read much about religion, though I do read the *Far East Mission Magazine*. It's more interesting than any sermon because it's about people who have given their lives to work for the Church, to help others.

Why don't they teach the Penny Catechism any more? I used to know the whole of it by heart and I always was first in the religious exams at school. An inspector from the church used to come to inspect the convent, and my mother told me when she came to fetch us that the nuns said, 'Mrs Hayes, we were so thankful to Patricia because the inspector suddenly descended on us and asked all these difficult questions which we'd never taught them or discussed, and up went her hand every time, and out she came with every answer, she was like a little Apostle.' But that was because my mother was a teacher in a Catholic school and she was always quoting the answers, so I learnt them from her.

I didn't find anything to disagree with in the New Catechism. It is very stark, black is black and white is white, but the truth is there. If you look at it carefully there's always a way out for people who can't swallow it. For example, like the teaching on missing Mass, supposing your mother says suddenly she's dying, what do you do? And the nuns would say, 'Always do the charitable thing. Go to Mass if you can but if you can't go because somebody's dying or sick then you can't.' I used to think it would be much better if there was more death and dying grandparents than the boring old religion! I cannot really find fault with the Catholic Church. It does have a ring of truth and other religions don't. But I don't think the Church is really fair to women, it doesn't appreciate them. Though of course it does appreciate our Blessed Lady, and puts her next to Christ, above all the priests and popes and everybody else, and that is very much in its favour.

I belong to the Catholic Stage Guild, because they won't let me 'un-join', rather like the Catholic Church. But I am interested in the Guild for its spiritual benefits. The annual day's retreat it runs is an excellent idea, and I would rather do it with a bunch of Catholics who are actors than with a bunch of Catholics who are not. It's a good day and we nearly always get a good priest. Priests get on well with actors because actors don't treat them like gods and they have a sense of humour. The other spiritual benefits of the Catholic Stage Guild are the Annual Mass and the fact that Mass will be said for you when you die.

I was married in a Catholic church, and the extraordinary thing was my husband, Val, became a Catholic through me introducing him to it. He had been a Communist and in the course of arguing about my views on Communism he started to read some Catholic stuff and decided to join the Church. He was so enthusiastic he literally forced his mother to become one too. She had always disliked Catholics, but he said, 'Because I am inside the true Church now I want you inside with me, Mummy.' So she started having instruction but did not get on with it. She protested a lot of the time, saying she didn't want to go to confession and to discuss her private sins with a stranger, she was also very against the rosary. I explained to her that it just puts you in mind of the whole of the life of Christ and you say a little prayer around each big event in his life and it is a good thing to do. When she told the priest that all her life she had disliked the very name of the rosary, he said, you can be a very good Catholic and never say it, but on the other hand he pointed out to her that it was a very powerful prayer. She thought she'd give it a try and now she won't go anywhere without her rosary.

I do think about religion a lot and always put forward the Catholic point of view when I talk to non-believers. I'm very impressed by people like Saint Bernadette who was so aware of the presence of God. I once said to a nun how I would wish to be like that and she said, 'My dear, you wouldn't like it if you were because you would be compelled to do all sorts of things that you didn't want to do. You are better being happy with who and what you are,' and on the whole I am.

Mary O'Hara

Harpist, singer and former Benedictine nun

I was born and brought up in the West of Ireland and, *ipso facto*, it was a Catholic upbringing. I never had any problem with practising religion; few people did in that context, but I never made any inquiries. It was not until I was in my twenties, when I met my first husband Richard, who died very young, that any need for questioning arose. That started the inquiry. Now, the older I get, the more I cherish what it is I have been given in the Faith, from my birth. Spiritual wealth and richness just pour out from the teaching of the Catholic Church.

I started to think more deeply about my faith because Richard was a genuine and deep seeker after truth. He was not a Catholic; he didn't adhere to any religion, but he was definitely very God-orientated. So, I felt that I had to explain my faith to him, and give him evidence for it. When he died, I knew, without a shadow of questioning, that I wanted to go into a monastery and give the rest of my life to God, in gratitude for all He had given me.

My husband's death made me far more aware of the Communion of Saints. We lose our loved ones, but they are lost in wonder, love and praise of God. Jesus said, on the night of the Last Supper; 'Unless I go, the Spirit cannot come', and when someone close to you dies, you get a totally new understanding of this. There is a joy. I must qualify that, because, at the time, you are torn to ribbons but, there is this tremendous paradox; you are riven with grief but, at the same time you are powerfully supported. You don't fall apart. You concentrate on what you know in the faith to be 'total bliss of the one you love', and when you concentrate on that your own sorrow and grief – which is healthy, of course – pales.

I have a deep and abiding gratitude to the Benedictine nuns at Stanbrook Abbey because of the spiritual openings which took place for me there. There was a tremendous 'sluicing out' of the Jansenism that was in my system as a result of my Irish Catholic upbringing. That was a great liberation. And so my years in Stanbrook were extremely precious.

Of course you can find deep spirituality outside religious orders. There are no barriers to the working of the Holy Spirit; 'it blows where it wills'. After twelve years at Stanbrook, I became very ill and began to realise that I should leave. My abbess put me in touch with a wonderful Scottish priest, Father 'Jock' Dalrymple, who has since died. After long and exhausting talks, and prayer with him, I was quite sure that to leave the convent was God's will for me. Once I was able to make that decision, peace flooded in; up to that it had been quite agonising; 'Do I, don't I? Will I, won't I?' I suppose if a person really wants to do what God wants, they will find it.

Isaiah, my favourite prophet, said; 'Whether you turn to the right or the left, your ears will hear these words behind you – "This is the way".' And, of course, we all need prayer. One of the Bible texts which I find most helpful is; 'The sheep who belong to me listen to my voice'. Listening is the most difficult thing to do, but that is a kernel text for me. 'God's loudest cry of love for us is in His silence, and God has veiled His love in the stillness of His silence.' In order to pray we need to be attentive, desirous, humble, waiting, still, and confident in our expectation.

Only now am I starting to understand what the Church is; not the institutional Church, but the Church as the Sacrament of Christ. I refrain from using the old term 'Mystical Body of Christ'. I always had difficulties with that. But *we are* the Church; baptised into his death and resurrection.

Then there is the Apostolic succession, and the witness, ongoing, unbroken. When I say the Creed, I believe every single item in it. Not only must we love the Lord with our whole heart and our whole soul and with all our strength, but, with all our mind, and constantly my spirit needs something more to develop itself, not simply to follow the teachings, the Fathers, and the theologians.

In spite of my convictions about God, I have certainly experienced doubts. Sometimes it seems that it cannot possibly be true. But that is when faith is called upon to operate in the presence of God. When doubts come, you use the 'muscle' that is faith, which, through exercise, has grown through the years.

I never think in terms of 'crosses'. Never. Everything is a gift. The old saying is true, 'every cloud has a silver lining'. There is no room for doom and gloom. Now it is the Resurrection that occupies my thoughts and my inner being – every day. I find the Resurrection a huge inspiration; joy overcoming gloom. It is so incredible it must be true. It is so fantastic!

Then there is the wonderful sacramental system. How could I be without that? The Catholic Church has it in its fullness. I couldn't be without the Eucharist; the sacrament of the Resurrection. In a marvellous way we are being assimilated into the risen body of Christ when we receive the Eucharist.

I often think that the Lord saw me coming out of the womb into the cradle and said; 'The poor little thing. She will never make it on her own. I'll make her a Catholic from the start.'

Edward Stourton

BBC newscaster

My father is very Catholic and very conscious of his Catholic background. My mother is Anglican in an Anglicanish way – church at Christmas and Easter – and while she was supportive, it was certainly my father who took care of our religious education. It wasn't religious in the sense that we said grace before every meal but it was certainly religious in that we were aware of it as a constant factor simply because we went to church every Sunday, which many other children at school didn't, and we were taught to say prayers in what I suppose now seems rather an antiquated way.

Perhaps I was an unduly trusting child – I remember being terribly shocked when my parents told me that Father Christmas didn't exist after all, because it meant for the first time that your parents could lie to you. They had told me that this person came down the chimney, so I suspect I was naturally disposed to take things on face value and accept the idea of the world that one got in church on Sundays, that my parents gave me, and that I got from my school.

I was at a Benedictine school and I found the monks immensely appealing. Even if you take Catholicism out of it, the Benedictine way of life has all sorts of strengths and gave you a feeling of being part of an institution with an enormous history. It's over 1500 years since Saint Benedict founded the order and in a gentle civilised way, the monks gave you that sense of belonging to an ancient and international tradition which had quietly preserved western civilisation. It was far bigger than any national tradition.

The great thing the Benedictine monks also do is to convey faith, but at the same time, tolerance. I remember when one of the monks was asked by a parent, 'Do you worry about the fact that some of the boys go home when they get to 17 or 18 and never bother to go to church and reject the whole thing?' He said, 'No, it's not the ones that do that we worry about, it's the ones who never challenge it.' So there was no sort of strait-jacket, not at all, rather Jesuitical if you like. Religion was there, but it was absorbed by osmosis rather than being forced down your throat.

I never questioned my faith but when you've been to a Catholic prep school and a Catholic public school where you have been basically happy and where you have absorbed the ethos, it's quite a shock at university when you suddenly realise that most people in the world are not Catholics. Obviously being a 19 or 20-year-old at Cambridge where everybody was having fun, including me, it's a very different atmosphere. Even those who were Catholics were certainly going through their rebellious stage so I don't think it was probably until then that I actually kicked against the bone – not particularly hard, but it would have been slightly unnatural if I hadn't. So it became rather an effort to go to Mass at the chaplaincy every Sunday. I never stopped altogether but certainly I became rather less rigorous about it. If you don't at some stage have a question mark in your head about whether God exists, particularly when you are studying philosophy and reading English poems it is odd. It is a question you can't answer. If it was answerable in an intellectual way it wouldn't be faith. One of the things that the Catholic Church gives you is that because of the discipline of being required to go to Mass every Sunday, you can't just put that question at the back of your mind and let it float away.

Having to go to Mass seems to me to be a good discipline. I have three children, of 12, 10 and 7. My 10-year-old and my 7-year-old do not like going to church on Sundays but, I am afraid, I just make them because it seems to me, at that stage, you are not grown up enough to make an informed decision. You need to absorb an understanding of what it's about. They both go to a non-Catholic school so they say, 'Sophie doesn't go to church, Tom doesn't go to church' and it is difficult to explain that they have to go. Also I do not think it is a particularly painful discipline. I say to them, 'It's just one hour a week, if that. You have to thank God for what you've got.' My eldest son is at a Catholic boarding school so he is, I think, sort of absorbing quite a lot of it anyway. Sometimes when he comes back after a weekend out, totally exhausted and he is fast asleep at ten o'clock in the morning, I do let him sleep in. I do not want to force him in a way that will put him off. He hasn't yet started to question his faith, but it will be interesting to see what one does when he is about 16 – if he says 'This is all nonsense, I'm not going to church' – and I don't know the answer to that. I suspect we will discuss it at great length.

I do not go in for teaching the children religion in any formal way. I think that one's principle duty is to provide them with an example of what a Catholic family can be like. At its best it is a family where there is an understanding that love is something more than a relationship between two human beings, that it is something that comes from God and is expressed in the way a family treat each other. You have to have the sense that the love comes from somewhere else and that it is bigger than you. It's not just that you are fond of each other, you are expressing a divine love in some way.

I think also, the Catholic objection to divorce is a helpful underpinning of family life. This sounds brutal but the fact that you know that you can't divorce, if you are going through a difficult time, then it is not an option in the way it is if you are not a Catholic. But I am not so in favour of Catholic teaching on contraception. That brings the authority of the Church into disrepute because people say, 'Look, this is just nonsense' and therefore distrust other things that bishops tell them. But, in general, the principle of discipline seems to me a very good one.

I would say the same about authority in the Church. The fact that you may disagree with a particular Pope doesn't undermine the authority of the Papacy itself. We all know that in the Middle Ages there were extremely badly behaved Popes and if you judge the Papacy by them, it's a complete nonsense. The principle of authority has to be tempered by tolerance otherwise you do bring that authority into disrepute and to a degree the authority depends on the consensus of the Church.

Another appealing thing about the Church is that it doesn't alter its stand simply because something is inconvenient, or awkward or difficult. Somewhere behind it is the idea of a church expressing an absolute truth. Of course all sorts of people do live in an admirable way without believing in God, or any church, but I just find, being intellectually rigorous, that I can't see anything to stop me behaving in a vile way if I wanted to if I did not believe that morality is founded on some kind of divine plan. I find it difficult to comprehend the idea of a moral structure without a Divine Being. Also, I feel that if you were choosing a religion on purely intellectual grounds, the Catholic Church has probably produced the most coherent way of simultaneously claiming to express an absolute truth which is divine, and living in the world at the same time.

Lots of other things attract me which are important but peripheral to the central question of faith. For example, I love good church music, I love boys choirs because I have heard them at school, and I still listen to the Benjamin Britten Missa Brevis in the car on the way to work at the BBC. I think it is beautiful and it evokes all sorts of memories, and I feel comfortable with them.

There is nothing particularly I would want to see change in the Church except perhaps the introduction of married priests. There must be all sorts of people who are married who would like to be priests and I am sure there are lots of priests who would like to be married and I don't really see any real arguments against it. I have more difficulty with women priests, perhaps because I am just conservative. Probably I have been pretty intellectually lazy about it for the simple reason that it doesn't seem to be an immediate prospect. The point about the Anglican decision was as much one about authority and setting yourself apart from the rest of the church and I think that is what upset a lot of traditional Anglicans.

One of the attractive things about being a member of a Catholic, whether a small 'c' or a big 'C', church is that wherever you are in the world you can always find a church to go into. Occasionally if I'm abroad, there will be some time when there's no filming booked or nothing is happening so I can wander down the road and pop into church. I did it recently in Cracow in that extraordinary church in the main square called St Mary's. It is the most stunning Gothic church and it was like stepping into an almost pre-Vatican-II Catholicism. The host in a monstrance was exposed on the altar and some twenty people in the side chapel were praying and various priests were waiting to hear confessions in the corner. Although you felt part of it, you also noticed that it was culturally different to your own experience.

My work does not really ever conflict with my faith. There is a slight difficulty with my habit of mind because as a

Catholic you are inevitably to a degree conditioned to respect authority and a large part of journalism is not respecting authority and suspecting it of doing all sorts of ghastly things. My faith does give me a consciousness of the moral dimension of stories I'm covering but I don't sit down in the morning and look at the newspapers and say, 'We must cover this, or that, because I'm a Catholic.' I do find a problem when I see natural disasters because that seems to be one area where the Church does have difficulty in providing an answer, whereas if one human being makes a choice to act in an evil way the Church has a way of explaining that.

For a short time I was involved in religious journalism when I began at ITN in the early 1980s. When the Pope came to Britain I was one of the few people around who knew what it was about and I remember writing a long script for Alistair Burnett trying to explain what transubstantiation was. It just happened as I had that expertise, and if you are trying to get on in journalism, expertise is very helpful. When Channel 4 news started I was sort of semi-official religious affairs correspondent. We did quite a lot on liberation theology which was very much a big deal then and I covered the Synod in Rome in 1985. Sometimes I write odd bits and pieces for Catholic magazines and I help with church things when I'm asked.

Various people have inspired me. One is my father, whom I admire immensely because he does a lot of quiet good work and his faith actually feeds the way he uses his time. I admire him immensely for what he basically is. People say, 'He seems saintly' and that may sound trite but he does. I admire Cardinal Hume for the way he has managed the Catholic Church in England and made himself such a prime spokesman for Christians in this country without it being offensively triumphalist and beating the Anglicans. When he speaks, people listen.

I was brought up with a strong sense of being part of a select tribe of Catholics who had kept the faith for four hundred years, ancestors who were martyrs and all that sort of thing. That was a great strength and one of the things that keeps the Catholic Church alive as it is, and one of the reasons Catholics in this country go to church. But the other side of that is the danger of it being a ghetto and enjoying that sense of being a religious elite, even taking pleasure in the problems of the Anglican Church particularly at the moment, with the possibility of more Anglicans becoming Catholics. The principle challenge of the English Catholic Church is to come out of its ghetto and become part of the main stream, and I hope it will.

Sue Ryder

Founder, the Sue Ryder Foundation for the Disabled, and widow of Group Captain Leonard Cheshire

My faith is the basis of all my work. I see the Ryder Foundation as a foundation of faith, and this has helped me to try, with others who have inspired me by their example, to assist so many adults and children and to realise that we must never lose faith, no matter how hard things may be. I cannot remember a time at which I did not have a faith and a deep trust in God. Nothing in my life could have happened except through God's will. Surely we are, as Pope John Paul has said, 'an Easter People'.

My parents were High Anglo-Catholics. The most influential was my mother. We lived near Leeds and she went to a Eucharist every day and we all went to church twice on Sundays. We also believed in the effectiveness of fasting and such things, many of which are now forgotten.

My mother had a reproduction of Millet's *Angelus*, of which she was particularly fond, hanging on the wall. Our childhood was strict and I never had the faintest doubt about the faith. Even when I was small, I remember visiting the slums with the district nurses. My mother was a social worker, and she and her friends used to raise funds for the installation of toilets or running water for the poor, and for outings away from the smog and the dreariness. The terrible conditions appalled me even then, but many slum-dwellers had such a strong faith themselves – even those who had fought in and survived the First World War. Many of them never blamed God for what happened.

When the Second World War was declared, I was 16, and I joined FANY, the First Aid Nursing Yeomanry, the first voluntary women's corps, registered in Britain in 1909. Somehow I was chosen during the first training course to serve in the Special Operations Executive. It had been created by Winston Churchill to coordinate the Resistance in German-occupied Europe. I worked mainly with the Poles. In so many ways they were so cheerful and courageous. Before that I was at a training station with the Norwegians, who were preparing for the attack on the heavy water plant in Norway, to prevent the Germans from developing the atom bomb *before* the Allies. After that I was a short time with the Czechs, including those who attacked Heydrich, the notorious Gestapo officer.

For all the rest of the war, I served with the Polish parachutists (specially chosen). The Poles had such superb faith and I am sure that it was very much due to them that I became a Roman Catholic. The transition was quite easy, and the Jesuit Priest who prepared and received me agreed.

When I think of those days, I am often reminded of King George VI's Christmas broadcast in 1939 and the quotation he used from Minnie Louise Haskins;

> I said to the man who stood at the gate of the year, 'Give me a light that I may tread safely into the unknown.' and he replied, 'Go out into the darkness and put your hand into the hand of God. That shall be to thee better than a light and safer than a known way.'

For believers, everything in life is ruled by, and decided by faith. I don't think I could have gone through all I did during the war years and afterwards without mine. I have seen such awful things, things that are past description. When innocent children were deliberately injured or starved to death, it caused some people to question their own faith, but I saw them as sharing in the sufferings of Christ. That is the only way I can answer it.

There was always so much to be done. Even when I met my husband-to-be, Group Captain Leonard Cheshire, we wondered if getting married might give us less time for our work. Before our engagement was announced we sent a joint note to our friends, in which we said;

> We believe that, with God's grace, we can now help each other cope more adequately than we have in the past, and wherever the work may take us we always look forward to keeping in personal touch with each of you. We do hope that our intention will receive your approval and that you will give us your blessing.

We were married by Cardinal Valerian Gracias on 5 April 1959 in his private chapel in Bombay which, in 1966, Pope Paul used during the Eucharistic Congress and Pope John Paul II too during his memorable visit to India. It was a simple wedding, as we meant it to be, attended only by a handful of close friends, and took place after my return to India from working in Poland and Czechoslovakia. The demands made on us were as heavy after our marriage as before, but we were able to bear much of the burden together. Our married life began with a joint undertaking, a tour of Australia and New Zealand, where we gave talks on our work in India and elsewhere, and raised funds for it.

What I like about the Roman Catholic faith is its unity and discipline. Alas, some of the discipline has been dropped, which I feel sad about. I deeply regret that we don't continue to offer prayers for the Royal Family, and for Russia. Leaving the decision as to whether to eat fish on Friday to the individual's conscience, I think was wrong. Many people are weak and will simply opt for what they like and what is easier. I even miss the genuflection which we were brought up to do during the Creed at Mass. I also regret the lack of fasting, and I am rather shocked when nuns, priests and other religious neglect to wear their habits or clerical dress and I have to say that I dislike it when the laity address clergy by their Christian names. It seems disrespectful.

There was a tremendous fervour and love of the Pope among the Poles. And particularly for the present Pope, John Paul II. He is so talented in his ability to speak so many languages. Before he was Pope he was in Crakow, as Bishop and, later, Cardinal. I remember meeting him when I went to his church in Poland, when he was parish priest. Even then, in the 1950s, you could see how impressive he was. He used to pray that he would see the end of Communism in Central and Eastern Europe. And, of course he has been enormously influential in all that has happened there both before and since the end of the regime. I am sure that he is longing to see the end of the brutal repression in China and Burma.

I was at all the Masses Pope John Paul celebrated on his first visit to Poland as Pope in 1979. They were most inspiring, with their seething crowds of millions. The high point for me was when a group of Auschwitz survivors asked me to join them at the Papal Mass at the site of the former camp there, and to go up with them to receive Holy Communion. I didn't think I should; I had not been a prisoner there. Beside me was a girl, who had been deported to Auschwitz at the age of sixteen, and she was in floods of tears. She could not ever have believed in 1941 that she would live to see the Papal flag, Our Lady's flag and the Polish Flag flying together from the SS watchtowers.

What would I like to see happen in the Church for the future? I think, because of the shortage of priests, that the laity will have to take on more responsibility for the Church and all it stands for. I feel greatly honoured to be a Minister of the Eucharist. It took me and my husband a whole year before we decided to accept Bishop Alan Clarke's invitation to accept the ministry. We felt that we might not be able to live up to the honour and the privilege.

I also wish that Church authorities could be more outspoken about social problems, like homelessness and the lack of housing which we have on a national scale. Unless something is done urgently it is going to get out of hand. For instance, if there were to be an earthquake, or if the Thames overflowed in London and great areas were under water, think of all the action groups that would spring up all over Britain to go to the aid of those people. But because homelessness is long-term and seems to be here to stay, the attitude expressed by some is, 'Oh, well, we can't do anything about it', or just to turn away.

Prayer has always been a great help to me. I spend three quarters of an hour each morning praying, from about a quarter to five. And the same in the evening. I enjoy reading the Treasury of the Holy Spirit and also I have a little book of prayers which I have collected throughout the years. I love the Litany of the Saints. As an Anglo-Catholic, I was brought up on litanies. Because I have moved about so much all my life, I do not need a special place in which to pray. I try to pray anywhere I happen to be. I even pray as I walk.

I really regret how secular and materialistic life has become in this country. God is hardly mentioned, not even in many schools. How are youngsters to learn right from wrong? They have no yardstick to measure things by. The majority are ignorant of Christianity, although they are often told about other faiths. Just because we have become a multi-faith society does not mean that we should desert our

Christian beliefs. Unfortunately we now have a generation of children whose parents know little about their faith and church teaching so are not in a position to hand it on.

However, I take great comfort in the large number of prayer-groups that have sprung up around the country. They are a sign of hope. Even in this country where there are over seven hundred abortions a day or to put it more plainly seven hundred murders, I still have hope in the revival of the faith.

I have always enjoyed the privilege of working with Christians from other denominations, and I have learnt much from them. The Foundation is interdenominational and members of the Sue Ryder Fellowship meet twice a year in the Foundation's Retreat House at Walsingham. Throughout the country Quiet Days are held in many of the Homes which bear my name or places of retreat, including a Scottish Church and an Anglican Retreat House.

I have a firm belief in the life to come. I am sure that if we have lived sinful lives we will have to go to Purgatory, because there is no justice on this earth, that's for sure. Those who have tried to do their best will enter Paradise.

I should like to quote a favourite prayer, written by Saint Bonaventure: 'Be not afflicted. In heaven I think of you. I love you. And, as in life, I am still with you.' My husband was both a great inspiration and companion. It was wonderful to have been able to share both prayer and faith with him for nearly forty years. And let me share with you the prayer he and I wrote together:

Usque Ad Mortem (Unto death)

To Thee, O my God,
Who art infinite love,
Yet who hast called us to be perfect, even as Thou art perfect:
Who so loved the World,
That Thou didst give us Thine only begotten Son,
And who hast thereby given Thine all, Thine everything;
Who emptied Thyself of Thy Glory,
And became obedient unto death,
Even the death of the cross,
For us;
To Thee,
We surrender our all, our everything,
To be consumed by the unquenchable fire of Thy love:
We desire to love Thee even as Thy own Mother loved Thee,
To be generous as Thou only art generous,
To give our all to Thee as Thou givest Thine to us;
Thou has called us, O Lord, and we have found Thee,
In the poor, the unwanted, and the suffering,
And there we will serve Thee,
Unto death.
Amen.

Charles Moore

Editor, 'Sunday Telegraph'

My decision to become Catholic was certainly no Damascus conversion. I had been thinking about it for a long time. Then the ordination of women crystalised the anxieties I had had about the Church of England. But I didn't think, oh, the Church of England is in favour of women priests, but the Church of Rome is against them, therefore I was going to the Church of Rome. These things aren't like party manifestos where you look and you see if you agree on a particular subject. I suppose I had been gradually getting more and more interested in the Catholic idea of a Church. I don't only mean Roman Catholic – I considered myself a Catholic within the Church of England. It doesn't make sense to talk about God except mediated through the authority of the Church. I cannot accept the Protestant view that you can do it by just talking directly to God and studying scripture. After all, how do you know what is scripture and what isn't? The very choice of what is the Holy Writ is made by an authority, and that authority is the Church. For a long time even though I felt that the Roman Catholic Church was the main part of the universal Church, I did not feel I had to be a member of it, because the Church of England was also a part of the whole. Then I saw that logically, because

I believed the Roman Catholic Church to be the main part, I should join it.

Initially, a lot of superficial things didn't attract me at all. Catholic churches are rather ugly. The aesthetic attraction on the whole is greater in the Church of England. But what drew me to the Catholic Church is its catholicity, that's to say, its universality. As soon as you realise that you are doing the same thing if you receive Communion in a Catholic church anywhere in the world, that has an enormously powerful effect on your mind. You do really believe that's how Christ intended it to be. The Church of England and clearly it isn't a universal Church in that sense and it is very divided about what actually happens when you take Communion.

I was brought up mildly anti-Catholic in the way that a lot of English people are. We thought Rome intolerant. When our Catholic friends made their first Communion at what Anglicans think of as a very early age we were shocked. But we did travel a lot on holidays on the Continent and our Protestantism never meant that we frowned on visiting Catholic churches. I liked them, they appealed to my sense of history. Also I read a lot and found there were people who became Catholics or who were always Catholics who impressed me, either by their holiness, like Saint Francis, or by their arguments, like Cardinal Newman. All this got me thinking about the Catholic Church and I did seriously consider being Catholic when I was at Cambridge, but I didn't do anything about it.

Once I became seriously interested I found several people who were very helpful, the Benedictine monks at Downside, priests at Westminster Cathedral, and so on. I am strongly attracted by the fact that the Catholic Church is so much a church for sinners and that absolutely anyone might be in it. I have always liked that aspect of going to Mass, really the whole of the human creation is there. It's almost an attraction of Catholicism that so many Catholics are often so bad. On the other hand the Church of England tends to have a slightly goody goody quality, though of course there are lots of Anglicans who are very serious about their religion.

Also I find the Catholic sacramental system crucial. I used to get in a rage because I'm afraid I'm very bad-tempered about the manner in which some Anglican clergymen conduct services, interrupting themselves or vulgarising it, or whatever. In fact, if I look at it objectively, some Catholic priests do this too, but I find them far less annoying because there's agreement about what's happening with the sacrament. It's rather like a surgeon operating on you. If he is the most affected, tiresome twerp, it doesn't matter so long as he can do the operation. In the same way the priest, no matter what he is like, is the man who can do the operation. Once you know that, your anger or frustration disappears, though a lot of cradle Catholics tell me how maddening they find their priests. I'm not starry-eyed about priests. I'm sure that many of them are not wonderful people, but their shortcomings don't get under my skin in a way that they did sometimes with Church of England clergy because I feel I'm getting to the sacrament itself, and they are just helping me get there.

The sacrament of Confession helps me a lot. I'm a bit irregular about it, but you do get quite a good signal I find, in your own mind, of when you really ought to go. It is also beneficial psychologically. Of course it can be abused. Some people say that it allows you to do anything and go and say sorry afterwards, and it can be played that way. But if the burden of anyone's sins is intolerable, it can't be borne by you alone, Confession constantly reminds you of the atonement and that the guilt has been borne by Christ for you. It doesn't let you off, but it makes it possible *a*) to live with yourself, and *b*) to know that you can only live with yourself through Christ and his sacrifice. I find that tremendously helpful. It doesn't matter much what the priest says to you when you're in the box, it's the fact that it's happening. Though I do on the whole like what they say in the box because it is usually simple. Often the priest just says a couple of sentences which sometimes are almost banal, and yet they can be just what you need to hear at that point.

Also I like having rules, so the fact that it's an obligation to go to Mass is a tremendous relief, and makes it far easier to go. I used constantly to think, 'Well, shall I bother to go to church or not', and I'd have a little mental struggle every Sunday. Now there's no struggle at all even if when you get there you may be in a rather irreligious mood or bored, or whatever, it's not a problem. And I like the general way the liturgy is conducted, even though the language is not beautiful and the singing is really atrocious, I suppose because there isn't a long tradition of congregational singing, and there are a lot of bad hymns.

When I was a child I felt the Catholic Church was rather foreign or un-English, but I haven't felt this for a long time. It is international in the good sense, and I much prefer the congregations. There are more young people, more mixed races, more poor and rich and middle and everything than in Anglican churches.

Because I like rules I do not mind the authority of the Church, although having authority is not the same as being dictatorial. It's a great liberation becoming a Catholic because I could only become one because I accept it as being true. That's the premise from which you start. There is the endless fascination of seeing how that truth is developed by intelligent people over the centuries, how it's applied in different times and developed in response to different questions. That's far more stimulating mentally and spiritually than when you're not sure what's true. It is not that sort of crude certainty that I sometimes associate with Evangelical Christians. It's a feeling that you've come to the right place, you're in the right building – as a metaphor, and as an actual physical fact. So you can get on with understanding.

The most important thing about trying to do that is praying, though I'm still very bad at it. Prayer is easier once you're a Catholic because you know what the framework is. You have a sense of how the prayer might be directed, what it might mean. I find the daily missal and certain basic prayer systems, like the rosary, very helpful. The great thing about ritualistic words is that they always have some effect even when you're hardly thinking. They have a constant meaning in which you sometimes strongly partake and sometimes you don't, but it's always there. One thing that's utterly confused and mistaken in people's view of Catholics is this idea that these types of prayer tend to make you superstitious and idolatrous. I find just the opposite, that they direct you towards what you should be thinking about.

One reason I'm not good at praying is that you need a peaceful disposition which I don't have. I read the Missal each night and fulfil the Sunday Mass obligation, and often I go into a church if I pass one. The trouble is, working in this wretched Docklands I don't pass one much.

As a Catholic you have to accept the Church's claim about what it is, and if you do that it follows that you try to live under its rules. So I don't have to go around constantly saying, 'Do I agree with the Assumption? Do I agree with the rules on contraception?' They are part of the teaching and I accept the authority behind it. It doesn't mean that everything's easy or attractive, and of course I'm just ignorant about a lot of the teaching. Some people seem to think that you are constantly being whipped into line by priests who lay down what you must think, rather like thought police. It is not like that at all.

Although I am very keen to accept authority, I dislike absolutism, and I think that the Church did go wrong from Pius IX, maybe earlier, over the insistence on the formal definition of infallibility. Though strictly speaking logical, this produced a rather hysterical mentality of opposition to reasonable independence and resistance to the modern world, which is silly. I don't think the Catholic Church is really like that, but it has had some of those elements. Over the years the Catholic Church's behaviour in the world is chequered, and I do not feel like justifying all the actions of the Vatican in history.

One of the ways that becoming a Catholic has changed me is that I'm less angry about religious matters. I used to get in a tremendous rage when I was an Anglican. So the change must be good, and I hope I am more tolerant for that reason. Also, if you feel that you are inside something which is basically coherent you don't constantly need to defend the position against attack. In the Church of England I was very factional, but I don't feel factional about the Roman Church, I just feel a member of it. Another thing I like is that the Roman Catholic Church is quite an adventure. It's not like being at home in the sense of being familiar, but for me it is the right place to be.

I used to think the post-Vatican II phrase describing the church as, 'The Pilgrim Church' was rather camp, but I now see that it does have meaning because it gives you a sense of movement, of going somewhere, and that you are constantly discovering more things. In that sense you're not in one place, although of course it has the rock-like quality that is always the same, but it helps you to develop in your own life, so you're not stationary.

One weakness in the Church I think is that those in charge have got too nervous about teaching people their faith. Many do not seem to get enough Catholic teaching and even when they do it is rather apologetic in the way it's done. But, under Cardinal Hume, the Church does seem to have developed a good place in English life. It is, as it were, coming out into broader society. It doesn't seem reactionary or locked in upon itself, or dominated by the Irish or any other nationality, it seems like a church should be – all things to all men.

When I wrote a piece about becoming a Catholic in the *Sunday Telegraph* I got far more letters than on any other subject. Most were favourable, though some were not. And it confirmed the view I've always had that religious subjects are greatly under-treated in the British media. People are more interested that you might think. The *Sunday Telegraph* has covered those subjects more than most newspapers and always benefited from that because it arouses interest and discussion and clearly relates to all other aspects of life. The idea that religion is a sort of curious hobby is obviously false.

The other thing about becoming a Catholic that does affect my professional life is that it does make you look at the way society is conducted with more amazement than before. For example, when all these protests about transporting veal calves were going on, I thought, this may be a cruel thing, but there is something mad, and I sometimes think we're really fairly mad in this country to be so worried about animals when so many foetuses are being killed in abortions, which is an infinitely bigger outrage.

When I'm writing comment in the paper I have to try to report the world as I see it, but I mustn't be sectarian. What I must do is not put a specifically Catholic point of view. This is what people are frightened about with the Catholic Church, they think you just take orders; I have to try to bring to bear a Catholic mind upon world affairs, which is quite different from getting the Catholic Church to tell me what to write. That is not usually a difficult distinction to make in practice.

It's an interesting problem and one that I'm aware of and I know it would be very damaging to the paper and an abuse of my position if I tried to turn it into a Catholic paper. I'm a Catholic editor, but this is not a Catholic newspaper.

Victoria Gillick

Mother of ten, campaigner and artist

I wasn't born a Catholic. My parents, in fact, were dedicated atheists and rather unconventional. They married in black in a Register Office just to show their contempt for religion. But my mother had great respect for the Catholic Church and actually had all five of her children baptised at one time. I was about 3 or 4 and my eldest brother 14 but she didn't become a Catholic till several years later, when I was a teenager.

She had been brought up without any faith and my father, who was twenty years older, was a lapsed Catholic. So she came a long way to be a Catholic but she was always reading, always interested in ideas, very stimulating, but a difficult and complex personality. She would have found atheism too boring. Once you have said 'There is nothing', then there is nothing else to say. No great literature has been written about atheism, it doesn't stimulate the arts or literature. The most creative and entertaining writers and artists have been Christians, and Catholics in particular. Her favourite authors included C. S. Lewis and G. K. Chesterton and people who have made that journey to faith themselves.

I don't know why it took her so long to become a Catholic. She used to go to church and obviously believed in it for us and wanted us to be in it, but she wasn't ready for it herself. Her marriage was not happy and by the time I was about 15 it was on the rocks. Our family had gone through a series of disasters. My father became bankrupt, our house had been burnt down, leaving us destitute. We had to go back and live in the burnt-out shell for a while and then moved in with friends. The family split up and the marriage fell to pieces. It was a terrible messy business and I think at that stage my mother wasn't ready to become a Catholic herself.

We went to a Catholic school and Mother taught us our prayers and came irregularly to Mass. Then she met some priests in London and they pushed her towards actually committing herself to be a Catholic. Throughout the upheavals of my early life, it was the regularity of going to church, the religious instruction, the ethos of the school which was the only stable thing. None of us lost our faith. It was very important, and I feel for the thousands of children whose families now break up and who haven't got any faith. They must be totally at sea. My faith helped me keep the balance in a stormy sea and it was terribly important.

Our headmistress, Sister Stevens, was terrific. The nuns at school were fierce but they actually did love you and you didn't realise how much until after your GCE's when they wrote you a nice letter saying 'I never thought you would make it', 'Well done', 'God bless you'. They really do care, maybe because you are their children. Obviously, some nuns have very difficult personalities and they would have been difficult personalities whether or not they had been nuns, but I enjoyed convent life.

I've kept journals ever since I was 14. When I read them to my children, they find them terribly funny because they realise nothing has changed. Teenagers in the 1950s are no different to teenagers today in the sense that you think everything's gone wrong. But reading what I was writing then, I see I was always thinking about my relationship with

God – whether or not this is the uncertainty of coming from a broken home and the need to be loved when everybody else's love was not certain – but the love of God was certain.

When I was at art school, I was never very good in discussion or in argument so I didn't really try to engage in it very much, it was really a question of 'Well that's my faith' and people left me to get on with it. One was very much in the minority. I went through a very sad phase and I lost my faith, though I didn't stop practising I just lost sight of God, I couldn't speak to him, I couldn't find him. I remember describing it in my journal as having slid down the side of a deep pit and I couldn't find the bottom, or the top, and just desperately looked for somebody to hold my hand and pull me up. I knew nothing then about the saints who have spoken of a similar thing – that dark night in the soul. It was only years later that I read about it and I thought, 'Yes I know what they felt'. These people went into that hole for years yet they still practised their faith and you find that you can too. Being at art school, I understood that you kept your exercises up, you didn't stop painting, or drawing or going through the daily routine. It was the same with one's faith so I didn't stop going to church.

That kept me in touch. You hear a lot youngsters saying, 'Why should I go to church, there's nothing in it for me?' I felt that, but I suppose the discipline of being sent to Mass and then the self-discipline in one's early teenage years of taking oneself to Mass stayed with me so that I didn't find it desperately difficult to go to Mass. It is all part of that duty that one has to God. It's rather the same as you feel about going to visit elderly relations. It is not enough to say, 'Well, I do love them but I don't need to go and see them.' Yes, you do. If the children are that reluctant about going to church, in the end there is nothing you can do, but if it is just a question of laziness, you have got to get them to go.

When I had experienced this loss of faith, I remember

sitting on a little hill in Cambridge and looking at the stars, very late at night and feeling so terribly alone and small and that there was nothing I could contact. If there was a Creator, I felt he did not know me. I remember coming back into the town feeling really lost and I passed by the big Catholic church, the Dollseye church as it's called, Our Lady and the Forty Martyrs, and going in and just crying my eyes out. People were bustling around and there was a lot of candle smoke going up and the light and the windows and the warmth and the smell and it just eased everything up and by the time I came out I knew I was loved again. It was as though somebody had actually come and put their arms around me and it was wonderful. I have never lost my faith to that extent again because I was always able to refer back to that and know that I had seen the truth.

A couple of years later when I had left art school, just prior to finishing my exams, and I had just gone off to Dublin, the nearest English-speaking town I could find that wasn't England, the same thing happened again. I felt I wasn't going anywhere, I didn't know what the future was, so I lost hope. I was about 19 and just walking down the street in the pouring rain – it always seemed to be raining when I was in Dublin, it was during the winter and the words came back to me from the 'Hail Holy Queen': 'Hail our life, our sweetness and our hope' and they suddenly struck me as absolutely beautiful and I just went along saying them over and over again and everything was lit up. Everything changed colour again and I just went back to my little bedsit and it was wonderful. I felt so happy.

I can't imagine being anything else than a Catholic because Catholics do seem to have this very straightforward relationship with God, with Christ, with Mary, and the saints. It's a very personal relationship and I find it is what I need and what many other people need. It goes on so many levels and seems to answer all the problems in life. By the time you are my age, you are also able to go back and be as a child with it. When I read the saints, I see their relationship with God is simple and straightforward and I can't imagine any other faith that has a relationship where God comes so close. I suppose I have stayed with it because God has stayed with me.

None of the Church's teaching has ever seemed very difficult to me. I have always been drawn towards its moral teaching instinctively, not because I have been particularly good but because it's become clearer and clearer to me that the Catholic Church has always been the place where you go when you have done wrong. It's not a church for people who have never done wrong, who have never failed, but a place where you find your home when you need it most.

Having had ten children, I've seen so clearly that a home is where you go to when things go wrong. When you have left home and you have made a mess of everything, you come back to that home. It isn't a place where only good children can live, and it is the same, it seemed to me, with the Catholic Church. When you are doing things right, it's marvellous. You can really expand and enjoy yourself but when things go wrong it's also your safe haven where you know you'll be forgiven and still be loved. And when things have gone wrong with the children, they have come back home to Gordon and me and know they won't be rejected. So many priests say nowadays that an awful lot of Catholics, when things have gone wrong, when marriages have failed, when they have gone off the rails, when they have been immoral, feel they cannot go back to church.

One of the difficult things for the vast majority of Catholics is their religious education stops when they leave school so their understanding of the Faith has never developed beyond that of a school child. Even quite intelligent people say, 'I don't believe in this Christian stuff, I don't believe in an old man with a beard and things.' Children need very simple rules but as they grow up you start to explain the purpose of them. If people do not get further training in their faith beyond school, they're still thinking in terms of a child and when they have done something wrong they believe they are going to be punished and that the Church doesn't love them because they remember the Church says that God will be angry with them and will not love them if they do something wrong. Now that's the language of childhood.

Adult formation in the faith is so necessary. Most Catholics don't read much about the Church and if the priests don't give them teaching in sermons and the opportunity to talk about it, it is very difficult. We are a very uneducated Catholic population yet we are besieged by a secular society that's hostile to Catholicism, and to any certainties or standards, so we do need the arguments to defend ourselves.

One area where there is certainly lack of understanding is sex – particularly contraception. I don't think the Church explains its stand in the language people can understand. I have spoken about it often to Catholic groups and I think there is a way of explaining it that makes sense. A lot of Church teaching is very masculine in that it is theological and when you consider that most Catholics don't have any great understanding of spirituality or theology, they are much more straightforward, then that is the only way to talk to them about it.

Having been involved in the whole controversy about contraception for the under 16s, I actually had to look at contraceptives and how they worked. Having done that, I'm convinced that the reason why they are wrong, is that they kill love. It doesn't matter whether you are married or not, the evidence is that relationships don't hold together when something at such a very deep level is being done to make the physical act of giving into a lie. From the point of view of somebody who paints pictures, it's an interesting activity putting paint on a canvas, but if there ain't no paint on your brush, the activity becomes pointless.

Nothing is being made. The same is true for sexual relationships. The couple are both giving something physical to one another but with contraception, one or the other, or both is rejecting the gift. Now you can do that while the excitement of the sexual act lasts, but not for long. For love to grow, it has to have all sorts of other virtues along with it which contraception actually denies. It's got to have perseverance, humour, patience and sympathy. Contraception cuts short a lot of those virtues so that's another reason why it doesn't help the relationship to grow.

When I was first having children, I only knew vaguely about how to avoid the most fertile times and Gordon and I practised it, sort of. We weren't desperate, we had lots of children, some with a gap of only about eighteen months between them. When natural family planning became more efficient, I wasn't particularly worried, I had five children under five so I thought in for a penny in for a pound. I wanted to have a large family so I might as well enjoy it. But a lot of people can't cope with that.

The whole point about fertility awareness and natural family planning is that it doesn't cut across the whole act of giving, it's not rejecting. It might be very difficult to find the humour that's needed to go with it and the self-restraint, but it's now so efficient that it's possible to practise family spacing with the fertile cycle so well that you don't need to have a football team.

It is difficult to hand on the faith to children in the same way as it is to hand on English or mathematics. You hope the schools will fill in all the details but that doesn't mean that you as a parent can't actually support the child in the devotional side, the actual, the reality of their relationship with God. Most parents, I find, don't say prayers with their children, not even simple ones like night time prayers or grace at meals, which is a simple devotional thing that binds a family so closely together. I have always said night time prayers with the children up to the age when I think they're able to say prayers themselves. At one time we used to all gather together in one room to pray. We always say 'Grace', we couldn't begin a meal without it. You feel as though something's been left off the menu. And we all go to Mass together. The three boys that are still at home are all altar servers still, even though the eldest is 23.

During the day I say the Angelus if I can remember. I was saying it this morning while I was mopping the blinking bathroom floor.

For the last third of my life I have been in conflict with either the government or various birth control organisations, even in court cases. Conflict puts your soul on the line. You are coming very close to actually hating your enemy, getting pleasure out of other people's downfalls. That's dangerous. I've come to accept now that my cross is to be the loser, whatever fight I get in. I have not managed, as far as I am aware, to change anything in my battles. One of my greatest inspirations was Josephine Butler from the last century, the one they called the forgotten saint, she was an Anglican and was the woman who fought for most of her life for the age of consent to be raised to 16 to stop child prostitutes. She was put through hell, she was physically attacked in trying to close brothels that traded in children. She wrote in her diary. 'There is a righteous anger that you can feel but it brings you so close to hell that you ask; "is it right?" "Will God save me in this position?"' And she felt herself close to the edge. In the end she came to the conclusion that the anger she felt was not wrong but she had to pray very hard to be steered away from that kind of anger. I felt myself in that same position and then one priest gave me some advice which I found has been very helpful. He said, 'Don't forget whenever you're going into any difficult situation where you are going to confront somebody, you pray to their guardian angels.'

The greatest help to my faith, indeed in my life, is my husband Gordon. I couldn't have survived either as a mother or as a protagonist, I couldn't have had a family or looked after them without him. He is so good with children, he is so good with me, he is terrific. Gordon has always helped me with my campaigns and has stopped me simply running away with my enthusiasm and forgetting my first responsibilities, which are to the family. He has been the great comforter, the one who said, 'It doesn't matter.' He helps me to get things in proportion and to stop me going off the wall, but I don't know if I've been much good to him.

One thing I should like to see in the Catholic Church is an improvement in liturgy. It should be more devotional, richer, fuller. I am confident that many young priests are coming through now who are aware that it is not a superficial enjoyment that attracts young people to the Church, it's a challenge, and a thorough understanding of their faith, not just of what they should be doing but why they are asked to do it. Some priests find it difficult to be the centre of so much attention, the Mass seems to depend upon their personality and they find that exhausting. Their faith may be strong but too much is being expected of them.

Also I find the music of the Church appalling. When the hymns are sung by terrific choirs, they sound great but when they are sung by your average person, like myself who's got not much of a voice, they sound awful. We have abandoned a beautiful art form and replaced it with something very shabby but then we abandoned an awful lot of very beautiful things in the 1960s and went in for a lot of very shabby stuff.

When you plod on you wonder what you are going to have to answer for at the end of your life and what your children are going to think of you at the end of it all, I know how you can judge your parents so wrongly when you're young. You just don't understand what motivates adults and it's only after they have died that you start to appreciate why they did the things they did.

Don Maclean

BBC Radio 2 presenter

I'm a Catholic because of three women really. Primarily my mother, who brought me up as a Catholic from a very early age. I liked going to church even as a small child. I suppose the theatrical being in me was already there and I just loved the whole idea. I still think as far as church-going is concerned we've got the rest beat. For a start our clergy have the best frocks and if you're bored by the priest it doesn't really matter because there's so much in the church to look at. There's all the statues, the crucifixes, stained glass windows, writing on the wall – it's in Latin, but it doesn't matter. It's a wonderful collection. Then there's other people doing what they're not supposed to, probably, and at High Mass if you've got big enough nostrils you can overdose on incense. It must have been awful to be an Anglican – because you sat there as a child surrounded by adults who seemed to know what they were saying. In my youth the Mass was in Latin so you knew that even the grown-ups didn't know what they were talking about.

When I was five I couldn't get into a Catholic school so I went to a non-Catholic one, but when I was six, the priest one Sunday announced that there would be religious instruction classes at the local convent for children who were not in

Catholic schools. So I turned up the next week on Saturday morning at the local convent, and met Sister Annuncia who was the biggest nun in the world. In those days nuns wore voluminous habits, so I didn't know whether there was a little thin woman or a big fat woman in there, but she seemed very tall, especially to a six-year-old. Her voice was like melted butter and she was just a wonderful woman. She was assisted by Miss King who was a primary school teacher. She's 88 now and she came to see me in pantomime twice at Christmas. They were both instrumental in giving me a really good grounding in the Faith and helped me know what I was supposed to believe.

I was the first child from the class to make my Holy Communion and I made it completely on my own, not with a group of children as is usually the case. I got to church in the morning and Sister Annuncia put a big dark red sash over my shoulder. Then I sat in the front pew and when time came to go to Communion I went up with Sister Annuncia, my mum and the Reverend Mother, a tiny French lady, who was always the first person to go to Communion at nine o'clock Mass every week. This time she stood back and let me go first.

When Napoleon was asked what was the greatest day of his life he said the day he made his first Holy Communion. For me it's a day that shines in my memory, far more than my confirmation. I found that boring, in Saint Chad's Cathedral with several hundred other boys and girls of my age, but there was something incredibly special about my first Holy Communion.

The Church, since then, has changed terribly, mainly because the Latin Mass has gone. I know everyone says the vernacular is important because we can understand everything that is said and I accept their arguments, but what distresses me is that, because of the change, and because of other things, Catholics seem to have lost their identity. As soon as the Mass was no longer in Latin and we could eat meat on a Friday we were no longer different. I think it was a major mistake to make those changes. I know it means we are getting more like other denominations, but when it comes to ecumenism the average Catholic says. 'That is great, as long as it's all under the Pope in Rome. I don't think any of us want to be Protestants.'

Of course there are good and positive things that came out of Vatican II. For example, the involvement of the laity in the readings at Mass is important, but I do still feel that we should have kept the Latin Mass. We have thrown something quite wonderful out of the window. People argue: why have the Mass in Latin just so that you can understand what is going on two weeks of the year while you are on holidays in Spain? But the word 'Catholic' means universal and as such the Church should have a universal language. My wife Toni and I went to Lourdes at Easter and attended Mass in the basilica. Several thousand people were there and seven priests walked up to the microphone in turn to say a little bit of the Mass in their own language. Everybody was bored. It was not a celebration of any sort. Then, the principal celebrant just stood there, stretched out his arms and said, 'Pater Noster' and the whole place joined in with the 'Our Father' in Latin. To me, that said it all.

Being a Catholic is the best thing that ever happened to me. I believe that the Church has an unbroken line back to Saint Peter. I know there has been a lot of talk about the corruption in the Church and the Vatican and how evil the Popes have been throughout history. But to me that says, what a marvellous church this is to have survived all those terrible people. There is no other institution, political or otherwise, that has lasted two thousand years. The Catholic Church has lasted that length of time and through most of its history it has done wonderful work and is still working for good throughout the world.

The Church's strength lies in the fact that it is reactionary.

For example, we have a very reactionary Pope at the moment and this is one reason why Anglicans who cannot cope with their Church are coming over to our Church in floods. I'm not just talking about clergy who are dissatisfied with the ordination of women, I'm talking about the laity as well. They are coming over because they're saying the Catholic Church is the one founded by Christ in the early days. We should keep it the way it was as much as we can.

Obviously we need to move with the times. Of course we need microphones on the altar. I also think the thorny subject of birth control has lost a tremendous number of people. When the pill was invented, the Pope had a marvellous opportunity to say we've been praying all these years for a natural form of birth control and here it is. God gives scientists the ability to create and to discover and surely the pill was a gift from God and should be used as such. I think it would have kept so many more of the faithful within the Church. You hear of nuns in Africa – when people ask them what people there need, they say 'contraception'. The big problem in so many parts of the undeveloped world is women being burdened with too many children, children they do not want.

But I do think the Catholic Church is right to refuse to ordain women. I am a reactionary and I would not be happy with the idea of women priests. Look at the damage it has done to the Anglicans. The Church of England is far too democratic. In our Church, if the Pope said we are going to ordain women next Thursday, everyone would say: I don't like that idea, but OK. Everybody has got to have their say in the Church of England and there are too many voices and that's why it's disappearing down a big hole.

My professional involvement with religion began four years ago when BBC religious broadcasting asked me to present 'Good Morning Sunday', the flagship religious radio programme. Honestly, I thought they must be raving mad.

I'm a comedian and why on earth did they want a comedian to present a religious programme? The programme had always been presented by a minister of the church and the last one was Roger Royle, a very good broadcaster. I think the programme producers felt they couldn't follow him with someone with whom he could be compared, and he certainly could not be compared with someone like me who has such a different background. We know the style works because we have doubled the audience and the programme now runs two hours instead an hour and a half.

I see my work with the BBC as a ministry and never in my wildest dreams did I think I would have a ministry, but I've got one now and I'm very jealous of it. I would like to do it for as long as I can possibly stand upright. I'm not trying to ram religion down people's throats – I simply never miss an opportunity to praise God on the programme and just say to people: God loves you, Jesus loves you. That's all.

I don't know if the programme is helping the Catholic Church because it's not just Christian-based. It's religious broadcasting for the whole country, so we talk about Buddhism, Hinduism, Sikhism, Islam, Judaism. Above all we are ecumenical. This experience has opened my mind tremendously. Until four years ago I only knew about Catholicism. That was a bit narrow but I could never be seduced by anything else I have learnt about. No other faith has moved me away from Roman Catholicism.

As a comedian I would like to see more humour in the Church, particularly in sermons. Many priests do not seem to realise that a bit of entertainment is a good way to get to children. We started going to a parish where everyone talked about their wonderful priest. The first week we took our children to Mass there, he started his sermon with a joke. The congregation laughed. My kids looked round. They'd never heard this before and from then on they were sold on him. If you can make people laugh they will listen, whether you're a teacher or priest or any kind of communicator.

Nothing turns people away from Christianity more than being po-faced. There must be a sense of humour. Are you telling me that Jesus travelled around the country with twelve young men in their late twenties early thirties and they didn't have a laugh? He must have been hilarious company. They must have had a great time.

Anne Widdicombe, MP

Government Minister

I became a Catholic on 21 April 1993. No one thing made me take this step, although the catalyst was the Church of England's decision to ordain women as priests. For many years I had been more and more attracted to Roman Catholicism. Perhaps I made a mistake in not becoming a Roman Catholic some time ago when I returned to active belief after a period of agnosticism. I am sorry in a way that I didn't take the step then, though I think its perfectly true to say that if the issue of women priests had not come along I might still be an Anglican, because I was very much an Anglican even though I was looking towards Rome.

One of the great attractions about Catholicism is its link with the early Church. What I found most difficult about Anglicanism, and indeed, about Protestantism in general, was the great gap between the Acts of the Apostles and modern-day practice. A huge lot was left out in between, whereas if you look at the traditions of the early Church you do get a lot of enlightenment. Protestants rely on scripture almost to the exclusion of almost everything else. As a Catholic, I have now found the early Church, which I certainly had not before. It does seem to me a little illogical, bearing in mind that it was a couple of centuries before anyone decided what the canon of Holy Writ was going to be, if you say that you can take account of the Epistles of Saint Paul or Saint Peter, but not of Clement of Alexandria or of the early Popes.

As an Anglican student at a convent school I was conscious of being in a minority and spent my time sticking up for the things I firmly believed. Those were, of course, pre-Vatican II days and there was a lot about the Catholic Church of which, quite bluntly, I disapproved, the exclusion of the people in favour of the priest, for instance. My favourite biblical quotation at the time was; 'The veil of the Holy of Holies was rent in twain' at the redemption and this seemed to mean that the people should have much more access to liturgical celebrations. Those were the days when the priest celebrated the Mass with his back to the people, who played almost no part in the process at all. Also I didn't like what I saw as a veritable superstition in the approach to statues and the saints and relics and all the rest of it; and certainly I queried the doctrine of indulgences, followed at that time. So intellectually, emotionally and theologically I rejected Catholicism in my teenage years.

The post-Vatican II Church in the 1960s was very different and that did attract me, though I must say that I do enjoy the Tridentine Mass occasionally. I regret the loss of the Latin language to the Church, particularly when I travel and I have to go out of my way to find an English-language celebration. In the past I could have gone to Mass in any church and it would have been in the same language. It made the Church universal rather than fragmented because the whole Church worshipped in the same language. Apart from that I do find Vatican II Catholicism much more attractive and much more 'livable-with'.

I also find the centralising tendency, with everything focused on Rome and the Pope, attractive after living with the other extreme, where virtually every Anglican bishop and every Anglican clergyman is able to come up with just about any variety of doctrine possible. Imagine the Pope, for example, querying the Virgin Birth and the Resurrection and still staying in his post! So I welcome a bit of central authority; I welcome Papal encyclicals and the discipline that is imposed by the Vatican. Sometimes I even wish it were stricter because I actually think that the Catholic Church is in danger of going down the same route as the others. And, while not wishing to return to a new Inquisition and total theological purity, I do think that a strong adherence, by its spokesmen and leaders, to what the Church teaches is no bad thing and a reasonable expectation.

I have often said, however, that if I had had no difficulty with some aspects of Roman Catholic doctrine I would have applied to Rome in November 1992, rather than in March 1993. Those intervening months were spent in resolving doctrinal difficulties, which I had to do because when you become a Catholic, you have to say, what no cradle Catholic is ever required to, that you accept all that the Roman Catholic Church teaches as revealed truth. If you are a cradle Catholic and if you have developed the odd doubt along the way, nothing specially to challenge your membership of the Catholic Church, that doesn't matter. But if you are crossing, and unless you are prepared to commit a fairly significant act of perjury, it actually does matter and you have to get to terms with all of it. That is difficult. And I found particularly the teaching on Purgatory difficult. The priest who was locked into these discussions with me expected me to find Papal infallibility a problem. I didn't. But the doctrine of Purgatory seemed appalling, challenging the completeness of Christ's redemption. It also seemed to suggest that there is some way that we could ever be good enough to stand in God's presence. The answer is that Christ's redemption has made what seems impossible,

possible. I eventually managed to resolve my problem by taking the line that if the Church teaches it, I will accept that it is revealed truth, even though I don't understand it.

I genuinely welcome the new *Catechism of the Catholic Church* and I think the to-do about the use of inclusive/exclusive language is a load of nonsense. If women have not realised, after all these centuries, that they are included in the term 'man', which applies to the race and not to a particular gender, then that is a severe indictment of their intelligence. There has never been any doubt whatsoever that we women are included in the general language that is used and I don't see the need to spell it out.

One area where the Catholic Church, and indeed all churches, seems weak is lack of involvement of the laity. The whole thing centres on a highly clericalised structure. If you ask yourself why, for example, does the Papal nuncio, the Pope's ambassador, have to be a priest? And if the job were to be done by a lay person there would seem to be no reason why it should not be a lay woman. The Anglicans asked, 'Why shouldn't women be priests?' and indeed, why should they not be bishops? Catholics are asking the same question, although coming to a different conclusion. The real question that we should be asking is: what role can the laity play, not as priests, but as persons within the Church? Certainly there are some functions that can and should only be performed by priests and, in my view, cannot be performed by women. But there are other functions, for example, at administrative or ambassadorial level, that could just as well be performed by women.

Becoming a Catholic has not changed my personal prayer-life much, though I do now invoke the Virgin and the saints: I still, bluntly, tend to 'go to the Boss', having spent most of my life doing that. The more free-ranging, Evangelical formats of prayer, in which I grew up, still attract me.

Like everybody else, I try to commit each day to God, and

to round it off with prayer. During the day, I frequently ask for guidance in decisions. In a sense, one's whole life is a form of prayer but I sometimes wonder if the Almighty might get tired with those of us who keep asking for help.

My reception into the Catholic Church, in a way, ran away completely. It became an utter media circus, which I had not anticipated. Not only did it occupy the national press almost to saturation point, but the international press as well. I had never expected coverage on such a scale. I felt it could be done quickly and in a very tailored way. I had never intended that it should be done in secret, but I did not intend the sheer scale of what happened. That was just one of those things that couldn't be stopped once the band-wagon took off.

When I left the Church of England, I was surprised at the number of people who wrote to me. They were feeling demoralised and they wanted to thank me for providing a voice on the issue of women priests. I knew that there were a lot of people in the Church of England who wanted to go over to Rome then, but who were not sure if they should go.

Several people have helped me a lot in my spiritual life. One is Julian Glazier, the MP for Canterbury, who is a Roman Catholic. Years before the women priests debate in the Church of England, I had been engaging in theological discussion with him on the subject of various Roman Catholic doctrines which I had found unacceptable. He always used to say that I would end up a Roman Catholic, and I told him that I would not. When I finally did, I said; 'There, you were right all along.' And he replied, 'Yes, but I never believed it, even when I was saying it.' He probably played a greater role than he realises.

Then I think Father Michael Seed, at Westminster Cathedral, the priest who actually bore the brunt of the change when he received me into the Catholic Church, played a major role, and so did Cardinal Hume. My contact with him was limited, but I did go to see him to discuss the Anglican situation in general in the period between leaving the Church of England and being received in the Catholic Church. At the end of that conversation he turned to my own particular decision, and some of the things he said (and it was a strictly private conversation) made a terrific impact on me.

The writings of Cardinal Newman did not influence me to change, but were certainly part of the background which gradually built up and against which I did change. Another thing that did bring me into closer contact with Catholicism was the abortion campaign. I have always been anti-abortion, but here the Anglican Church seemed to lack leadership completely. My time in the convent school did not make me consider becoming a Catholic though it did do all sorts of other things for me and for which I will be eternally grateful, including introducing me to the general Christian ethic and putting God first in my life.

Bruce Kent

Peace campaigner, CND

All my education and background, you might say the 'climate' in which I was brought up, was Catholic. That is the world I know and that is why I am a Catholic. I remain one because there is no better home to go to. I believe in the message of the Gospel, and that Christianity is a community affair. The Church is a community trying to follow the Gospel, and I need that community. Certainly I see now, much more clearly that I did when I was younger, the deformities and the warts of the Catholic Church, but I see similar ones in the other churches, yet the love of Christ shines through all of them, but I wouldn't dream of moving. However, I now consider myself first a Christian and then a Catholic. Whereas, when I was 25, I should have said I was a Catholic first, and then a Christian. The Church at its best is a light to the world; a model of fairness and virtue, simplicity, poverty and openness. This is God's message to the world and the world should want to live this life. Of course, this is an ideal, but even now there are patches of the Church where it is like that. I don't know where else you could go to get the same kind of vision and fellowship that you find, for example, in the Pax Christi movement or in the Catholic Worker movement, or in the Justice and Peace groups or with the Archbishop Romeros and Franz Jagerstatters of this world.

I don't know where else I should ever be able to find three hundred people, from all parts of the world and from every class, in fellowship as I find every Sunday in my local Catholic church. Not even the Labour Party has such a rich selection of people; Asians, Philipinos, West Indians. Our parish may not be a great model of vibrant social change, but it is a place where all sorts of people meet, irrespective of class country or culture; and I treasure that.

Historically, of course, the Church is an international movement with all its missionary enterprise. It also has that flavour of independence which you do not find in the Church of England, which, and this may be a brash thing to say, seems too concerned with its own national status. This is not true of the Catholic Church. I also think that the Irish aspect of the Church in this country is exciting. They have a generosity and an openness affecting their style of religion which I find attractive. Yet I do have greater rapport with people in other churches than I have with many in my own. I don't suppose Cardinal Ratzinger and I would be on speaking terms, for instance, but I am very friendly with (the Anglican) Archbishop Trevor Huddleston. I have also found much to admire in the Methodist Church and the Church of England. But I stay in my Church because I belong to the bit of Christianity that I have always belonged to, and I see no reason why I should change.

The Catholic Church is secretive in terms of its administration and it can be difficult to find out how things are being done. I find that frustrating. In the Westminster diocese at the moment few people know who makes decisions about money or have an idea about the extent of property owned by the Church. Financial accounts do come out, perhaps every year and a half or two years, but in a form that no accountant would look at seriously.

Certainly the religious life of the Catholic church is attractive and the contemplative orders are impressive.

These are people who have stepped out of the ordinary way of doing things in the world and devoted themselves to God and to prayer. Yet they are not remote, they are concerned with what we others are doing.

I like belonging to a really international Christian community, which the Catholic Church certainly is. On the other hand, I am disappointed in the way the Catholic hierarchies of England and Wales, though not of Scotland, are so bound by structures which regularly support the British Establishment.

My own vocation to the priesthood began during a retreat just after I left the Jesuit college of Stonyhurst. We were asked to examine our lives and to consider what God might want us to do. I could almost sense the great finger of God reaching down to me – like the Lottery posters! This seized me and I could think of nothing else. I still retain that sense of destiny and feel that I am doing what God wants in my work for peace and disarmament.

For the five or six years before I decided to leave the active priesthood I was deeply unhappy because I was not getting the support for my peace work that I thought I was entitled to. I wanted the Church to be in the forefront of that work and it wasn't. When I was made 'Man of the Year' by the BBC Radio programme Today in 1983 for my peace work, I didn't get a word from any of the hierarchy. You would think that someone could have said 'Well done'. Not a line from any of the bishops. So, although the people in the parish where I lived were very kind, I was always aware that I was an outsider to the official Church. When the bishops did say something about disarmament, I was never consulted, although I was a Catholic who knew as much about it as anyone else. It was then I realised that the Church authorities were only tolerating me and I felt I was a square peg in a round hole.

I was also lonely, though my life was very busy. People

asked whether I left the priesthood to get married. No, I did not, although I am now happily married. The decision to leave came to me almost like a spotlight. It was November 1986. The election of 1987 was coming up, and I knew that the 'priests and politics' issue would start up again. I realised that I was waiting for the bishops to order me to leave CND. I knew that if they did that I should refuse to obey them. I was actually waiting for them to ask me to do something that I wasn't going to do. It was a dishonest position to be in. That really was what made me make up my mind to resign. And I was right. There was a great sigh of relief, I can tell you, when I announced that I was resigning. Clearly I had taken a burden off the episcopal backs and no impediment of any kind was put in the way of my departure.

Having made my decision, I found that I was into financial insecurity, which I had never experienced before. I actually had to work out how I was going to live. For example, who was going to pay the bills? This was a new concept for someone who had been supported by church collections, week after week.

Now I see myself as a retired priest. I have not asked for laicisation because I do not believe that my work is not that of a priest. People accept me for what I am. In my autobiography I tell the story of the old man who lives round the corner and who came to me one day and said; 'Monsignor, be careful, there are photographers trying to get a picture of your wife.' He obviously was not concerned about my status in Canon Law.

These days lots of 'fringe' people come to me about funerals, or new babies or other events in their lives, asking me to put some kind of ceremony together for them. For example, some time ago I went to the cremation of an elderly Communist. He was a man who believed in justice and truth. His wife came to me when he died and together we worked out a ceremony to mark his death. Another person recently came to me who had just had a new baby. She and her partner were not into church-going, but they asked me to arrange a ceremony for the child, which I did. So I now find myself fulfilling a priestly role for people who, perhaps, would not accept ordinary priests. That is quite moving.

I wish the church authorities would wind the clock back to the Liverpool congress of 1980 and see what it proposed. It was a great moment of hope. It was not very radical. There were discussions about money, clerical appointments, the causes of poverty and the place of women in the Church. In all this there was consultation and participation. We all thought the changes promised by Vatican II were going ahead. But the whole thing was soon ignored.

Unfortunately, the tragedy of the last twenty-five years is that many of the lively minds in the Church have now departed and left us with a rather dull organisation. All that the rest of us, who have stayed, can do is to go on challenging. We need to create our own networks where we can meet and discuss. For example, I saw a recent conference on 'Why I am still a Catholic' set up by a number of fringe bodies, including a group of Catholic lesbians. All sorts of fringe Catholic things are going on and I think this is good.

If you ask 'What is the symbol of this age?' The Lottery? The supermarket? We have a madhouse of shopping, seven days a week. Does the Church have anything to say about that? We have spent thirty *billion* pounds on Trident. The campaign against the arms trade was founded in 1973, yet there is no regular subsidy from the Catholic Church towards it. The Methodists put in £500, a year, the Quakers £2000. The Church of England central administration also puts in nothing. There is no point in talking if we are not prepared to take action as well.

My concerns, these days, are very much with what the

Synod of Bishops called the sins committed against our society. In other words, the structures of greed, power, violence and obsessive nationalism which have done and still do so much harm to humanity. Too often, the Church is more concerned with sexual sins than with the corporate sins of unjust structures in society. Many in our Church seem to think that politics has nothing to do with religion, except, of course, when it comes to Communism.

The Church would gain a lot if it brought in the marginal people like myself. Hundreds and thousands of married priests, and even some bishops, throughout the world could do so much. At the moment, many of them are embittered because they are cut off. Yet they are still part of the family and should be made to feel it.

Hardly a day goes by that I do not spent ten or fifteen minutes in prayer. Prayer is very important because it focuses your eyes with God's eyes. It cleans the window from the inside to see God's world and to see yourself as the creature of an almighty creator who has a plan for you in that world.

My favourite saint is Dorothy Day, founder of the Catholic Worker Movement. She is not canonised, of course, but she is an extraordinary woman, conservative in liturgy, radical in politics. She has set up homes all over America for the poorest of the poor and she did more to make the American Church into a peace-making church than anybody else. Others who have inspired me are: the former Archbishop of Bombay, Tommy Roberts, who was such a strong influence on me. Here was this transparently stubborn, honest little man who challenged the traditional Church on hard-line interpretations of moral teaching. Other heroes are Desmond Tutu and Trevor Huddleston (a personal friend). In the 1980s I was deeply impressed by Edward Thompson the historian, so passionately dedicated to peace in Europe. He had a lovely sense of humour.

In one lifetime I have already had more than my share of privileges. Above all, I have been blessed with the love of friends and with a sense of purpose which has never faded. For both, I am profoundly grateful.

Mary Kenny

Journalist

I was very much brought up an Irish Catholic. In the 1950s when I was growing up in Dublin, Catholic instruction wasn't so much imparted as absorbed. Doctrine was not knocked into you, it was all round you, part of the culture. They say that faith is caught, not taught. The notion that Catholics were indoctrinated in the past is entirely false. For example, when I began to think about a question like abortion I came across an article saying; 'Of course, Catholics are indoctrinated from birth about abortion'. But in our generation it was never even mentioned because it simply was not contemplated. Of course, we were educated in the Catholic faith at our convent school. My family regarded religion as natural, but were not 'holy Joes'. In Irish Catholicism there was a healthy strain of mocking a person who was over-pious. They were said to be 'eating the altar-rails'. My brother told me that in the west of Ireland, where he went for summer holidays in the 1940s, even grown men liked to put out their foot and trip people up as they went to Holy Communion. They thought it was funny and that people always trotting up to Holy Communion were showing off. For me, religion was just a natural part of life. My parents were extremely easy-going, sort of 'bourgeois Bohemian'. They were very interested in the arts and that sort of thing, but were not very practical about things like money. Their attitude was 'live and let live'. So they were very far from being rigid or zealous Catholics.

Going to Mass was taken for granted. Everybody went and you said the rosary and all sorts of other prayers. It never bothered me and I just went along with it. But by the time I was a teenager I was in full rebellion against everything. I was always a very naughty girl and a difficult child. So I was always questioning authority. Some people say to me the Catholic Church completely repressed all opposition and squeezed out individuality, but it didn't. It did not oppress my opposition or keep my voice out. I felt well able to talk back and to give cheek and the rest of it.

I was very bold indeed. I suppose it rather came to a head with the contraception issue in the sixties, although, quite honestly, the first time where I really felt in opposition to the Church was when I went to France in the sixties when I was a young woman and there was a controversy about the Pope and the Jews, which has been raised again now. There was a famous play called *The Deputy* by Rolf Hochhuth. It was playing in Paris and it was a tremendous shock to me. I was part of the generation that was just learning about the Second World War and the horrors committed and this play alleged the Pope had done nothing about it. When you are young things seem so black and white. Although now I appreciate more the difficulties, I still think he could have shown a bit more bravery.

The other thing about age, is you learn more humility and you begin to wonder: how brave would I have been? That was brought home to me by Christabel Bielenberg's experiences. She said if you hid Jews the Nazis would simply take away your children or your family and torture them or shoot them. So you just didn't get involved.

I was an au pair in Paris, but I was also studying at the

Alliance Française and became very interested in all sorts of protest movements which were starting. Later in the sixties when I was in London and then in Dublin it was 'the pill' issue which surfaced with *Humanae Vitae* which made me protest. I thought it was absolutely absurd that the Vatican should be so antediluvian about this. It seemed perfectly simple that women should be able to control their fertility. Of course, I felt even more strongly about Ireland – where birth control was banned by law. The Irish had inherited a Victorian British law about birth control which had never been revoked. What was actually banned in Ireland were barrier devices but the pill didn't fall under that ban simply because it was a medication – it was technically different. So even to this day you see books saying the pill was banned in Ireland. It was not, but birth control devices were. It seemed to me absurd that a government should be telling people what to do in their bedrooms. However, again, I now see how much more complex these issues are and I've read a lot of material about human life. I actually think now that although women should have the possibility of fertility control, there is enormous abuse of birth control. Also a lot of things that the early birth control campaigners like Marie Stopes believed would happen, haven't. For example, Marie Stopes predicted that the breakdown of marriage would diminish, because people would be much happier as they wouldn't be worried about pregnancy. But just the opposite has happened.

The second thing that those early birth controllers said, was that there would be no such thing as criminal abortion of any kind in the future because people would be able to control their fertility so well. That hasn't happened either. So in those two important aspects the birth controllers have been proved wrong and some aspects of the Catholic position have been shown to be very wise.

During my protest years I became a sort of Marxist. I was

very interested in Marxist ideas and feminism and so on. I would never do anything as passive as 'lapse'. Either I would be anti-Catholic or very pro.

Broadly, although I always have secretly quite liked the atmosphere of a Catholic church, I suppose what brought me back to it was growing older and having children and also maybe my mother's prayers; I don't know, because I had some very, very delinquent phases in my life. Also I had a big problem with drink and almost became a destructive alcoholic. It must have been prayers or something which suddenly helped me end that. Although it seemed to be sudden, when I look back I see that things happened gradually.

Sometimes also you learn things from the most unexpected sources, not necessarily from the very holy person you think will teach you something, although you learn something from everybody. The former editor of *Private Eye,* Richard Ingrams, was asked why should people be religious and he said, 'Religion is natural to man.' This struck me as very true. One realises too in reading history how many efforts have been made to destroy the Church by the French Revolution, the Industrial Revolution, the Modernist revolution, Freudianism, Marxism, feminism, socialism, fascism, and totalitarianism, and it is staggering how Catholicism has simply survived.

As I said, religion is natural and I find that Catholicism is the most coherent expression of it. I feel very much at home with it and I also feel that although it's seen as very authoritarian and orthodox, there is a lot of variation and elasticity in a curious way. There are all kinds of different Catholic people and churches and yet there is a universality. That mixture suits me well.

My father nearly became a Jesuit. He studied in the American seminary in Beirut and was very influenced by the idea of the universality of Catholicism, how we were linked with Poles and Spaniards and the Portuguese Empire.

Then I find the devotional aspect of it fills my spiritual needs. My prayer life tends to be irregular. There are times when I go through very 'unprayerful' periods when I feel completely uninspired about prayer. One of the saints once compared prayer to writing. They said if you pray, keep praying and you will learn to pray: keep writing and you will learn to write. Maybe there is an interesting parallel there, because with writing you can't just wait until you get inspiration. You have to be fairly methodical and actually keep doing it, and I suspect the same applies to prayer. One of the things I miss and I think I should try to do something about it, is some kind of collective prayer, like the rosary, and taking part in a rosary circle or something like that. I used to find that very inspirational and it helped me through moments when I wasn't feeling prayerful.

All this is not to say that I am not highly critical of some aspects of Catholicism. For example, the fact that Catholics don't always live up to the ideals of the Church, behaving badly in business and so on. If you are supposed to be a Catholic or Christian you shouldn't jolly well behave like a cad in business. You should just try to keep the Ten Commandments.

I am married to an Anglican and I have read a lot about the Irish Protestant tradition of trying to bring an ethical dimension into everyday life and trying to be honest. All these things are very difficult. I do think that it is an ideal maybe Catholics sometimes lack.

David Alton, MP

Human rights campaigner

I'm a cradle Catholic and I was baptised in a Franciscan church in the East End of London. A couple of years ago I was invited back to that church to give out prizes at the local Catholic school and afterwards I was asked if I would like to see the baptismal register. So I went into the church of Saint Anthony accompanied by an elderly priest who found the entry. I asked whatever happened to Father Andrew who had baptised me and he said, 'That's me.' So not only was I a cradle Catholic but I had a chance of meeting the priest who'd done the job.

My mother is a devout Catholic from a traditional Irish Catholic family. She came to this country from County Mayo just after the war with all the simple faith that people from that part of the world have to this day, and that communicated itself to me. My father had been in the Church of England, but his brother was killed in the RAF during the war and my father partly blamed God and became hostile to the Church. At best he was agnostic, at times atheistic, though he mellowed a lot. He died a year ago. And I felt towards the end of his life that he had come a lot closer to God. I was very touched to find after his death that one of the things he had made my sister only the year before was a small wooden Celtic cross.

So it was a family with tensions. There had been tension about my mother, a Catholic marrying a non-Catholic, and I was particularly touched that my father's funeral was held in the Catholic church where they had been married. My father-in-law, who is a retired Anglican priest, conducted the service with a Catholic priest participating, reading the lessons and welcoming the mourners. It was a lovely moment of reconciliation and I think my father would have been very pleased to see that the old animosities had very much been buried.

Prayer was important to our family and I've always believed in the old Catholic saying that the family that prays together stays together. Your faith is built up by a combination of upbringing, the example of your parents, other people you meet and your school environment. My primary school was run by the Sisters of Mercy who were wonderful. I have nothing but happy memories of that time and the sisters had a huge influence on me. One reason why I am still happy to spend a lot of time with religious sisters is because they are such extraordinarily good people. Fortunately, in Liverpool where we live, our next door neighbours are the Poor Servants of the Mother of God, who care for handicapped women there, I couldn't wish for better neighbours; they remind me in many ways of the nuns who taught me. At eleven I went to a new boys' Jesuit grammar school which had just opened in Essex – Edmund Campion School. The spiritual dimension there and the concern for justice deeply influenced me and I've always retained a fondness for the Society of Jesus for that reason. I became the sacristan which meant I'd often come in very early in the mornings, getting up at half past six, taking a bus and a train then walking to school to serve Mass in the community. There was the compensation of a huge cooked breakfast after Mass, so it wasn't all holiness. It was also the thrill of even for just half an hour being part of the Jesuit community there and I was very sad when they left.

One of my first political actions was to organise a petition in the school which we took to the bishop demanding that they send us a chaplain. We even said who we wanted. We were effective because the priest that we asked for, a Jesuit, was sent back to the school to act as our chaplain. He was also an enthusiastic teacher. The only subjects in which I excelled at school were the subjects in which I was encouraged by teachers and where my confidence was built up. In subjects where I was told I was hopeless, I lost interest. When I was about fourteen I told him that I thought I wanted to become a priest and he did his best to dissuade me. He encouraged in me a sense of discernment and to seek out what it really was God wanted me to do. I knew God wanted me to do something with my life.

Many people leave the Church because they are not helped through that period of growing up but I was very fortunate that the people I encountered in the institutional Church always gave me a lot of support and encouragement. When I went to Liverpool it was to a Catholic College and I deliberately chose to study divinity as well as history to keep open my options as to what I might do subsequently. In fact, it was politics that I got immersed in because that was where my faith led me.

For two years I taught in a Catholic school in Kirkby called English Martyrs. The children called it 'English tomatoes'. Then I worked for five years with children with special needs – handicapped, disabled or maladjusted. It was demanding and challenging but I could happily have gone on doing it for ever. But while I was at college I got involved in local politics and as a final year student was elected on to the city council and then I stood for Parliament and in 1979 I was elected as an MP so that ended my teaching career.

I believe in Providence and I think God has a plan for us all, but he gives us free will so we can either choose what he wants or reject it. People talk a lot today about 'my right to choose'. These are murderously loaded words. G. K. Chesterton once said on the theme of choice that 'to admire mere choice is to refuse to choose'. Simply saying we are free to do whatever we like is a nonsense, because that leads to selfishness, sinfulness and anarchy. Whereas if you choose what God wants for you then you won't go wrong.

Discernment is the only way you can try and find what this is and often it will be only when you look back that you will know where you took the right turning and the wrong one. Prayer, the study of scripture and listening to God are the only way to discover His will. There's no short cut. For instance, my constituency has been abolished for the second time in my term in Parliament and looking at the boundaries I can't see any point in contesting any of the seats that have been created in Liverpool. I have got to try to work out what God is saying to me in all that. Maybe the answer is not the answer that I want. Maybe it's that there is something else to go on to.

Often we pray, but we tell God the answer we want. We don't accept that 'Thy will be done' at all. We want our own will to be done. If God wants me to stay in Parliament and in politics then a way will be found.

Some people say it was Ignatius, others Augustine, who recommended that we should pray as if the entire outcome depends on God and work as if the entire outcome depends on us. I think that is the sort of motto that politicians should have nailed upon their door. It is essential to find time every day for prayer, not just on your knees or in contemplation, it can also be in the ordinary things you do. Prayer can be offered in short gasps as well as in long ritual. Most of what you do in your life can be some form of prayer.

I usually go to the Christian Fellowship which meets at

the House of Commons on Tuesdays to study scripture and pray together, for each other's intentions. It's just one small window each week but it's a good time to spend with others of different denominations. Every day Parliament begins with prayer and MPs turn and face the wall while they pray. This dates back to a time when MPs were even worse behaved than they are today. They poked tongues out at one another regularly and distracted each other during prayer so they now turn and face the wall. Also we have a Catholic Group in Parliament which I have helped to establish, and Mass is offered regularly in the Crypt Chapel. Sometimes I try and take a couple of days for private retreat. Perhaps a little time in a religious community just to recharge my batteries. We all need to do that. Joyce Huggett wrote a brilliant book called *Listening to God*, where she said we all need to be contemplative, charismatic and evangelical Christians if we are going to be properly rounded in our faith.

Politics itself is not a dirty business, but some of the players do have dirty hands. That's true of everything in life. If people come with the wrong motives it diminishes the whole process, but for the Catholic who believes strongly in public service and the social teachings of the Church, there is no choice but to be involved in public life. Religion is not something to privatise. You can't pretend the rest of the world doesn't exist. Jesus himself talked about the need for us to be the salt and light of society. That may mean that people despise and ridicule you and there is a danger that when you affirm your faith in any kind of public way people will accuse you of being either a hypocrite or a sinner. Well, surprise, surprise, we are hypocrites, we are sinners, because that's human nature. At least we're aiming for what remains a very noble ideal. One of our problems today is that people aren't encouraged to aim for the ideal. Nor are they encouraged to think about repentance and contrition which seem important to me for a person's well-being.

Every day is a new day. We can start again, however much emotional baggage we bring with us, or however much sinfulness, that does not mean that we are rejected from the body of Christ. The Church talks about how we all make up the body of Christ. I prefer to think of us as the handicapped body of Christ, his disabled body, because all of us are disabled or handicapped in some way. We try to pretend we are not and the world encourages us to think that we can be perfect. Even the amniocentesis test from the very moment of conception, and other procedures that are being developed to check if the unborn child is normal encourage people to think that you can destroy what does not measure up to somebody else's quality control.

Read the opening chapters of Saint Luke's gospel. I think they are the most moving in the entire Bible. Here was Luke, who was a doctor, obviously an intimate of Mary's and she must have confided in him the most sensitive and personal details about her pregnancy. I am always moved when I read the story of how the tiny embryo that Jesus then was, was greeted by a tiny foetus, John, who jumped in his mother's previously infertile womb. That story is bypassed in so many Christian narratives. Jesus came as all of us come, first as an embryo who became a foetus. The Psalmist writes that each of us was known in our mother's womb even before God had made us. I believe that each person is unique and made in the image of God. This gift of life from God is not something that we have the right to throw away. For me it's the supreme human rights issue and I campaign vigorously all over the world, about this and others issues such as poverty and injustice in areas like my own inner city constituency in Liverpool. But I would be a hypocrite if I didn't also care about the most vulnerable of our species, the unborn child. It is hypocritical to care about the awful things we do to calves as we transport them on ships, if we do not also care for the human before it's born. This isn't a question of being anti-abortion, it's about being positively pro-life and caring for every human being from the moment of conception to the moment of death.

Catholics in Britain have a great record for protecting the unborn, the vulnerable women who are exploited by men and the infirm and dying, but there is always more we can do. We must always make it clear we are not trying to judge. We want to cherish both the woman and her child. People's thinking about these issues must be changed. The Catholic approach is not popular, but Jesus was not very popular either. After all, when the mob were offered the choice of either him or Barabbas, they chose Barabbas, the violent political leader, and they crucified Jesus. So his followers now shouldn't expect to be praised by contemporary commentators. They may be rejected, so what.

Certainly I have had my crosses as a Catholic. All of us find that there are times when Church teaching is either difficult or it doesn't fit in with what we want. For instance, I was very sad that when Lizzy (who is not a Catholic) and I married, we weren't able to have a nuptial Mass where we would have had inter-communion. So rather than having a Mass where only half of us could receive Communion we decided it was better not to have the Mass at all. That was painful. When our children were born I would have liked my father-in-law to have been able to baptise them. He's fifty years an Anglican priest but Catholic Church rules didn't permit this. Maybe those rules will be changed. I encourage the process of change but I do accept authority and obedience, even when it causes personal anguish and pain. Catholics are fortunate in having the Apostolic Succession, and in having the Pope as such a cultural guide, even though some teaching can seem hard from time to time.

One area where I think the Church could develop is in the use of married deacons and eventually ordaining them to the priesthood. But I do think we should continue to choose our bishops from celibates because we uphold celibacy as being, as Saint Paul says, 'the greatest calling', if you are capable of it.

Also women's ministry is crucial. I do not accept the criticisms sometimes made of the Catholic Church, that it's full of misogynists and is unable to recognise the importance of women. My experience of the Catholic Church is that it is remarkable women who help to keep it running. Look at Mother Teresa or Mary Ward. Personally I do not support the ordination of women – not because there are any theological problems, but because if it leads to the kind of division that the Church of England has experienced then it cannot be good for the Church.

My middle name is Patrick and I enormously admire Saint Patrick because he combined so many qualities. As a young man he experienced being separated from his family and so many people today experience the break-up of their families. As a young slave, he was exploited and yet he came to love the people who had exploited him. That shows enormous generosity. As an Irish citizen as well as a British one I feel sad about the hatred in Ireland and I think that Patrick – as someone from Britain going to Ireland – showed a sense of love that should be shared amongst all people. He was a great evangelist, he spared himself nothing in walking the length and breadth of the island in order to convert all of it. He had great faith – he believed in miracles and there were miracles surrounding him. His legacy has inspired generations of Irish people to go out and serve the Church in the world and I think he is underestimated as one of the really great saints.

I have received so much from the Church, from earliest childhood that I have nothing but love and affection for it. Of course it's not perfect, how can it be, we are all sinners. So the Church does fail from time to time, sometimes very publicly and that causes us all anguish, but we should remember that we are all the Church and if we don't like the quality of our parish, then it is our job to contribute, to use our gifts to assist in its development and growth.

Also the Church has done so much for human rights. Look at the stand it has taken in countries such as those of Eastern Europe, where I have travelled widely, where there have been tyrannies and totalitarian regimes. Those of us who have been privileged to be brought up inside the Catholic Church should not be tempted away. A seed grows best where it has been planted.

Lady Rachel Billington

Novelist and journalist

I am actually not quite a lifelong Catholic because my parents converted when I was about three or four, so I was born an Anglican. My older brothers and sisters were given the choice of religion because they were in their teens when my mother became a Catholic, as my father had earlier. I was brought up in a convert atmosphere, which I think was a bit different to growing up in a family which had always been Catholic. It wasn't like being on the inside of the Catholic Church.

My first schools included two convents in London and a couple of years in a non-Catholic school in the country, run by a friend of my mother's. Then, at eleven, I went to the newly founded convent of More House and I think my time there has a lot to do with my attitude to Catholicism. Now it is mostly run by lay teachers but then there was an inspiring headmistress, Reverend Mother Veronica. She was very individualistic and didn't believe in people following the herd – she used to pull us out of line at the morning assembly, saying, 'What do you think you are? Sheep!' We believed that she really wanted to be a missionary in Africa and found us middle-class girls quite dull. She taught maths and was a very clever woman. So the atmosphere of the school was unlike most convents, in the 50s. Religion was not thrust down our throats at all. We went to Mass once a term and did our pretty pictures of grapes which turned into wine, then into the blood of Christ, but we were not told that we *must* do things very much. Rules and regulations did not really come into the picture and the school proudly boasted of having no formal rules. Instead, we were encouraged to take responsibility for our own behaviour. Of course, it was still a very small school; I was the twenty-seventh pupil to join.

I was not a very religious child, like some of my friends who had been at some of these strict boarding schools, such as Mayfield and others. They used to fall on their knees to say their prayers at great length and they all went through a phase of feeling that God was calling them. I was quite afraid that God would call me. Religion did not concern me deeply, I just felt it set out an acceptable way of behaving. But the Gospels and the life of Jesus fascinated me and continue to be my real interest, and have been subjects for some of my books.

Like most people then, and probably now, the moment when I thought about why I was a Catholic and wondered if I truly was one, arrived when I was about 18. I went to university and started to face the question and the realisation that the Church's teaching of no sex before marriage put me out of line with my peers. In those days, many of us Catholics were thrown into a trauma of terrible guilt. Many of my friends left the Catholic Church then and didn't come back, which is very sad. As for myself, I didn't fall away from Catholicism with a bang, rather with a whimper. I continued to go to church sometimes and to believe that the Church set the best possible ideal of good behaviour. But I did find it difficult to reconcile its teaching with my wish to be free and open to new ideas. This was the sixties, after all! Not that I can pretend I was ever seriously wild. Although my father was a very staunch Catholic, I can't remember any conversation with him during that period. But both my parents have always believed in teaching through example rather than with heavy discipline. Besides, when I went home I did go to church, so my parents probably weren't very aware of the state of my faith. Also, I was living in New York for much of the time.

My adherence to the Church returned in the conventional way when I got married. I was introduced to my husband by Malcolm Muggeridge and I had no idea, nor did Malcolm, that Kevin was also a Catholic, even though they had made a documentary together about Cardinal Heenan. Later, Malcolm became godfather to our daughter Rose, and ten years later, she was there when he, too, became a Catholic.

Before the wedding, Kevin and I had some sort of instruction at Farm Street church and I said I wanted a nuptial Mass. The sympathetic priest, called Father Nevin, explained that we couldn't have one unless we were both Catholics. At which point, Kevin revealed he was a Catholic too so it was not until then I discovered I was marrying a Catholic. Kevin had been brought up Catholic in the North of England and was, and probably is, more of a traditional Catholic than I am. So we did have a nuptial Mass and got back to the Church on a regular basis. We had four children and we were both keen to bring them up as Catholics which meant that we would have to go to church every Sunday as an example. In fact. I'm sure we would have gone anyway. Now they're 24, 22, 19 and 15. None of them went to Catholic schools, except the youngest, but they had Catholic instruction and would all definitely say they are Catholic. Some of them go regularly to church, others less so. I feel it is their choice after they are eighteen but I am very happy when they do attend Mass.

One aspect of the Church I find very difficult is that it is a huge and formal organisation. As a writer, you desperately need to be able to approach things independently and individually, so for me, Catholic belief is more directly to do with what I take to be the Church as I find it in the teaching of Christ in the Gospels.

This is especially true when it comes to sexual morality. One of the most important aspects of the teaching for me again comes from scripture, that is, the importance of forgiveness. Along with love, this is to me the basic Christian message and I find it difficult when I come into contact with certain people in the Catholic Church who, as far as I can make out, seem to favour punishment more than forgiveness. I was recently at a debate organised by the Westminster Cathedral Club, and I found to my amazement many of these good Catholics were very keen to condemn more, which meant more punishment, more prison. Luckily I didn't discover their views on capital punishment, where the Church has not had a good record, at least in the past, though the Pope does now seem to be taking a stand against the death penalty.

But what I do like is the way the Church emphasises that each individual being is equal and has an equal chance of doing good, experiencing joy and happiness. This was not so evident in the church I grew up in but it is certainly what Jesus taught.

It is possible I might not have been a Catholic, were it not that I was virtually born one. Having said that, I'm very proud of calling myself Catholic and couldn't consider any other church, so my attitude is not exactly straightforward. For instance, I would call myself a left-wing Catholic and I admire the Church when it's involved with liberation theology in South America, but I'm not so happy when it starts interfering too closely in matters such as birth control which I feel should be left to the conscience of the individual.

Last autumn I was reading the Pope's book of interviews, *Threshold of Hope.* In fact, I reviewed the chapter about youth for *The Tablet.* I approached it with some anxiety, fearing it would be dictatorial and condemning. It wasn't. On the contrary, the Pope explained how he looks with the greatest hope towards the young because they are the section of society most filled with idealism. It was an inspiring chapter. The Pope did not raise the subject of sexual behaviour and I like to hope (not with much justification, I fear) that, by emphasising the high principles of many young Catholics, and by not mentioning sex, he was allowing that it's not of primary importance.

The area where I believe the Church needs to do more is with the young and this means better communication on an individual basis between priests and young people in an open and sympathetic way. If the young person feels they are going to be cast out of the fold when he or she is in a state of sin, often because of sexual relationships, they see two alternatives, either to toe the line or to leave the Church voluntarily. By a sexual relationship, I mean of course not a general promiscuity, but two people coming together in a loving and responsible way. If such a person is encouraged to stay in contact with the Church by a priest and continues coming to Mass, there will still be the problem about whether he takes communion or not. Ironically, the most high-minded are the most likely to stay away altogether, unwilling to act in a hypocritical way and telling themselves, 'I'm breaking this rule so I can't be part of it at all.' The result is that many young people are not getting any nourishment from Catholicism at this most important time in their development. I know many young people who face this dilemma.

Yet, as the Pope says, these are the best of our society, the future for the Church. There is no easy answer but I feel we should at least be talking about it honestly. Even those people who do return to the Church at a later time have missed out on contact with their religion at the age when it is most natural to be thinking about attitudes to life and faith, as they are about their careers. They may never approach religion in quite the same energetic way again.

An important moment in my faith was when I started writing children's books on religion: *The First Christmas, The First Easter* and *The First Miracles.* I had to go back and study the Gospels of Mathew, Mark, Luke and John. What really struck me, re-reading them as an adult, was how totally inadequate most of the disciples were most of the time. I think we are given a consoling, even cheering, message by their failures. Again, it's about the whole question of forgiveness. They let Jesus down constantly, misunderstood him, underrated him and finally abandoned him in his hour of need, but, far from condemning them, Jesus made them the pillars of his Church.

Clearly, if you have a Church which is laying down rules which are very difficult for most people, that colours the way we read the actual stories of Jesus' life. It makes it possible to miss the fact that they're filled with humour, irony and, above all, anecdotes of human relationships. The most vivid, I notice, are often when women play a central part. For example, when one reads Martha's scolding reaction to Jesus' late arrival after she has summoned him to Lazarus' bedside, it makes it impossible to think of Jesus as a remote holy person. Similarly, there is Jesus' hen-pecked reaction to Mary's request at the marriage feast of Cana. The closeness of his relationship with the various women in his life seems even clearer when they are the ones who stay with him at his crucifixion, and then his first appearance on Easter Day (if you read the right Gospel) is to Mary Magdalen.

Another area which I would dare to suggest the Church should be thinking about is the nature and image of Mary. Now that feminism of the most positive sort, that is, a recognition that men and women should be allowed equal aspirations in all areas, is more or less with us, her old image as mother, and nothing more than mother needs a bit of an update – in my view anyway. And, as I've already suggested, there's plenty of grounds in the Gospels for thinking she was anything but 'meek and mild'.

Although I go to church regularly, I don't get very involved in parish activities, but I hope my writing helps Catholicism in some small way. If you ask me about running the Church then I'd suggest it should have various tiers of clergy: celibates, probably monks, a tier of married priests, which after all the Church did have up till a thousand years ago, and, of course, women priests.

I am not very good about prayer and too often my prayers are asking for something – I'm famously successful with Saint Anthony – but I try and have a few calm moments when I think how my behaviour might fit in with a higher being. That, I suppose, is a kind of prayer. I don't often say formal prayers such as Hail Marys or Our Fathers, but I very often make resolutions, and break them.

A Catholic upbringing has been helpful to me as writer because it has given me a moral framework. Although I don't find the teaching easy, my belief in a firm code of morals from which my characters may deviate or not, makes writing more complicated and therefore more exciting. Although in no obvious sense 'Catholic novels', I think my books have often been about the clash between freedom, independence, self-fulfilment or whatever you want to call it, with moral duties which find their strongest expression in the rules of the Catholic Church. A few years ago, I wrote a novel called *Occasion of Sin*, about a married woman's love affair, which Father Ronald Rolheiser told me he used when teaching courses on marriage. My most recent novel, *Bodily Harm*, which is the double story of an aggressor and a victim, was dubbed 'controversial' because the victim so far forgave her attacker as to become his lover. But as I said, forgiveness is very important to me and I've always felt there should be no limit to it.

Non-Catholics sometimes assume if you're Catholic life is easier because things are decided for you. It's not like that for me at all. People talk about the great peace and joy of faith but I can't say I've found that, perhaps because I haven't worked hard enough at it. Or perhaps it's because of my profession. On bad days, I do feel that, far from being a help, my Catholicism is a severe limitation on my writing. Sometimes I feel I'd just like a day off to know what it feels like! However, when I'm writing my religious books, I have been happily surprised by a sense that I'm being given special help from somewhere.

Overall, I am aware of having taken a tremendous amount from Catholicism and I have a guilty sense of not having given enough back to it. I hope there's still time to do that.

Dr Jack Dominian

Psychiatrist, author and founder of 'One Plus One' charity

If you believe in a continuity from Jesus through the Apostles, I am persuaded that the Catholic Church is at the centre of this continuity, and so by belonging to it one links up with the Lord in the fullest way that one can as a Christian.

I think that, at its best, and I live in a parish which is at its best, the Church can be a community of love. For me, the Church is not about belonging to an institution or about rules and regulations or authority. It is primarily meant to be a community of love. Its priests and its religious are at their best, really, when they foster that. The rules and regulations of the last three hundred years are the remnants of a church in which the relationships between the clergy and the lay people, the bishops and the clergy, and the Pope and the clergy were really more those of parents to children. We began to grow away from that model of church at the Second Vatican Council.

Under the present papacy we have stalled and there has been an attempt to return to the older model, but it is a model that we have outgrown and we have to become a community of mature adult Christians. Of course, this will be under a central aegis of the Pope, but living in a pluralism which really has to be much more marked than it is at present. The present Pope, John Paul II, is a figure of contradiction. He is popular, and yet there are those who openly contradict some of his teachings. Certainly, in America young people think highly of him and respect him, as I do myself, yet, at the same time they perceive some of his views as simply wrong.

We have got to get back to the roots of the Second Vatican Council, which started a journey towards maturity and growth, but which I think frightened the Church to the point that it stalled. But the Church must trust people and educate them for a mature life. What you see in many Catholics is a mature intellect and body and sometimes mature emotions, but a child's spirituality. This has to alter.

At the heart of Christianity there is a relationship with the Blessed Trinity, in which we are incorporated in a mature relationship with the Godhead itself. We must not mistake the institutional Church for God. The Church is there to nurture our relationship with God, not to replace Him. Too many people think of the Church as their end goal. It is not. The end goal is the mystical Church; the Mystical Body of Christ in which, at the heart of being a Catholic, is love; loving God and loving your neighbour. Everybody, from the Pope down, must be a servant of love.

I am a cradle-Catholic. But a radically changed one. I was very conservative until the sixties, and then, slowly, I began to change and really to grow up and mature. This came about through my work with the Catholic Marriage Advisory Council. I was brought up to believe that if you did all the things that the Church told you to: no premarital sex, marrying in church, avoiding contraception and adultery, going to church every Sunday, then you were expected to have a perfect marriage. But in the CMAC I saw that lots of people had done all these things, but their marriages were in tatters. So I began to question the wisdom of this type of teaching on the nature of marriage and I started writing about marriage not being a contract but being a relationship. I suppose, I began to grow up and have a true dialogue with the teaching Church; the type of dialogue that the best theologians always had with it, but as lay people very few of us had experienced.

I never thought of leaving the Church because I have always been convinced that it is the Mystical Body of Christ and my faith in Him has always been deep and penetrating. But I did begin to realise that the teaching Church had and has many limitations. Because of this, to some Catholics I am anathema; not acceptable at all because, like children, they want to think that the 'parent' is the only authority. But you cannot idealise. You have got to accept the Church with all its limitations.

My work with the charity One Plus One centres on marriage. I have seen and heard so much about marriage difficulties from so many kinds of people that I am convinced the Church must hold on to the doctrine of indissolubility. This teaching comes directly from Our Lord himself and I do not agree with those theologians who try to water down this ideal, On the other hand, I think that we have not paid enough attention to preparation and support for marriage. The Church has uplifted the single state to a tremendous degree, and yet 90 per cent of Catholics marry. In a nutshell, we have not taken marriage as seriously as we should.

Preparation for marriage is very important. But it is not enough. We have got to support the newly-married. The Church has so often concentrated on the wedding. But that is only the beginning of a journey in which the Church must accompany the couple throughout their married life, which nowadays can span fifty years or more. It is no good having a tight discipline on divorce if we do not have a commensurate plan for training and support for married couples.

With regard to contraception, it is not, whatever the right wing of the Church claims, an infallible teaching, and I see no basic problem in modifying it. I am not saying that natural family planning may not be a very good way of doing things. But I do say that the ban on artificial means of contraception, as presently held, is untenable. We have tried, for twenty years, to find a reasonable explanation for it, and we have failed. The teaching on this has to change because it really does no justice to the Church.

The basic doctrine that every sexual act should be open to the possibility of fertilisation has no foundation whatsoever. I think that the Church must get round to recognising this. I would say that the primary purpose of sex is to seal the unity of the couple. We glimpse the life to come through our loving relationships on earth. At the present we have a philosophy that intercourse is both creative (for the relationship) and also pro-creative. I don't think that that is so in western society. The primary purpose of sexual intercourse is the unity of the couple, to foster dialogue, and I think that the biological side, procreation, is of very limited application. One of my great frustrations, in the last twenty five years, is that we have wasted so much of our energy on the subject of contraception that we have not been able to spell out a positive message on sexuality and marriage.

I have no problem in holding these views and continuing to be a practising Catholic. The Church is an evolving church and I am sure that the last word as not been said. The last word on love will only be uttered on the Last Day, because love is the nature of God, and only at the end of the world will we fully understand love.

The link between sex and guilt belongs to an earlier generation. Younger people today, in their twenties, thirties and even forties, no longer connect sex and guilt. They have a much more open understanding of sex. We may have gone 'over the line' in many ways in the last thirty years, but we have learned to understand human sexuality so much better than we did in previous generations. Sex is the signature of love in a relationship. It should not be used to explore relationships. It should be used to seal them. And when they are sealed, it should be used to sustain the relationship and help it heal and grow. The present madness about sexual trivialisation cannot last, because it is so destructive and tragic. I think that in protecting the dignity of sex, the Church is absolutely right.

My father was a Catholic, my mother was Greek Orthodox, and although she converted to Rome, she remained very much Greek Orthodox at heart. I lived in Athens until I was 12, then I went to India for four years. I came to England in 1945 so, this year, I shall have been here for fifty years. So much of my adult life has been influenced by the Catholicism of this country. But my own growth and change did not have much to do with where I or my family were. It was a change that took place within myself.

As a psychiatrist, I have been very conscious that the generation of Catholics I grew up with were not mature. Although they had grown up in other ways, they had not matured spiritually and they were very attached to the keeping of rules and regulations, like attending Sunday Mass. I hope for a Church in which love will replace authority, in which the scriptures would displace authority and in which a community of love would displace a hierarchical structure. I have been very frustrated in the last fifteen years that we have not moved more in this direction.

In recent years I have been very fortunate to have, as my parish priest, Father Jim Duffy. He has helped me to understand the importance of the Word of God, and of the consecration of the Eucharist as really re-living the Last Supper and as an act of love for Our Lord.

Otherwise, I find prayer, personal prayer, difficult. For me, loving my neighbour is the centre of my prayer-life. I have a 'triangular' notion of God. You are aware of Him, and through that awareness you love your neighbour and through loving your neighbour you are aware of God. But loving, which is at the heart of our faith, is such a difficult thing to do that we get distracted by liturgy, by rules and regulations, by obedience and authority at the expense of loving.

To help me develop my faith, I like to read *The Tablet* each week, and I am fascinated by Christology and have many books on Our Lord. I am trying to understand the mystery of the Incarnation in terms of love and I am busy writing a book on that.

Among the people who inspired me was the late John Todd, who was my publisher and a very spiritual man. My spiritual home is the Dominican centre, Spode House. I went there after Vatican II, both to lecture and to attend conferences. I would also have to say, with great respect, I think Cardinal Hume is an exceptionally spiritual man.

I am very inspired by many of the saints because they have lived a life of love to the full. For me, Saint Thomas More is a special person. He gave his life out of love for the truth.

Today I am far more contented than I was in the past, because, as I explained, I do see a vision of the Church as a community of love, which is really thrilling, and which links us to the life to come.

What happens to us after death? I think we will receive a deeper sense of God-as-love, and our own loving relationships with one another will deepen. But you get a good idea of how things will be even in this life. All our failures, pains, triumphs and successes share something of Jesus' life, death and resurrection.

Richard Coles

Former pop-singer

I have not been a Catholic long, and I am still wearing L-plates. I was brought up nominally Anglican, and I can remember, as an eight-year old chorister, getting up a petition to say that people who did not believe in God should not be made to go to chapel. I was a thorough-going, rigorous atheist. But like most Bolshevik atheists, I was never far away from Christianity.

Coming from the gay community in London in the 1980s, and as an active socialist, I would seem to have been light years away from Catholicism. But the people and influences most powerful in my life when I was younger – people from the Young Communist League, those working in gay liberation – many of them had a Catholic background. I think Catholic social teaching has plenty to attract anyone interested in justice. Two of the people who had most influence on me had been brought up Catholic. They lived by a vision that gave them an ability to see that we could achieve something better. And I think their Catholicism had given them an optimism. Religious faith enables you to have hope and joy. You'd be mad to turn your nose up at that.

My grandfather, who used to make me hold my nose when we walked past the Catholic Church (in case I inhaled incense and developed popish habits), had thought deeply about religion. He had that quality of vision of something glorious which lay beyond the everyday realities of life. It took years for me to realise that was available to me too, and it has become available through the sacraments of the Church.

When I stopped working with the Communards in 1988 I thought I'd have a year off, just read, settle down in my new London house and think about the future. I was about 25 and had lots of money. I took about every pharmaceutical substance you could get. That was also when AIDS was making its impact in my life and those of my friends – a few died. If you're in those circumstances when death and sickness are constantly on the agenda, I don't think you are ever very far from religious consideration. I got in a dreadful mess, and decided to get myself into shape.

After I first started getting religious twinges I went to a psychiatrist who told me to go and see a priest (Anglican), so I did. With enormous tact, patience and intelligence, he provided me with the means to get on with life. When I got to my late twenties I became curious about Christianity, curiosity turned into something deeper, and I found myself in the position where I needed to embrace it. My first contact with the Church was with Anglo-Catholics, at Saint Alban's, Holborn, where there was a wonderful liturgy and some extraordinary people, but for me it was not home. I met a waitress in a restaurant in Islington. She said she knew a priest at Buckfast Abbey. We started writing to each other, and have since become friends (he is now the Abbot, David Charlesworth). He was a person who would put up with the wild and fairly silly things that a person like me – from gay, socialist, alternative London – would say, and with patience. I've found with people who have had an influence on me – it's not so much what they say, but what they are. Part of the value, which I think is inestimable, of contemplative nuns and monks is that they live out their vocations for the benefit of the rest of us. I took instruction and was received into the Catholic Church at Pentecost 1992 in Buckfast Abbey.

If there was one thing that made up my mind, it was the desire for sacraments. If you don't eat, you get hungry. If you don't drink, you get thirsty. If you don't breathe, you suffocate – and it really did feel like that. When I first went to Mass I entered as a spectator and left as a participant. I saw myself, as a Catholic, sustained by the sacraments and in a community with others, as a way I could be happy and fulfilled. I saw a vision of a future for myself, and for everybody, that seemed something worth pursuing and making sacrifices for. And it has made me very happy.

Some of my friends were horrified – particularly at the fact that as a gay man, I had become a Catholic. I understand why they thought that. They see you are not mad, and that you are enjoying yourself. Hopefully, being a member of the Church changes you and perhaps they have noticed the change. It's made me happy, given me – through prayer and through the Mass – the chance to take up a place in the community of the Church and be able to possess that vision glorious. To have that in your life is transforming and wonderful. And there is such a hunger for it. It's about understanding what it is to really be human – to live as God created you, being open to other people, generous with yourself, and allowing other people to be generous around you.

I decided to do a theology degree at King's College, London because I was curious and wanted to get to grips with the intellectual side of Christianity. It was three wonderful years. As I had a clichéd view of Christianity I thought I'd be the only person there with my background. But Christianity penetrates surprising places. I discovered that in the year above me at King's had been the saxophonist from Roxy Music, and in my year was George Hargreaves, a Pentecostalist minister, who had written a whole load of hits for Sinitta. It was almost a trend . . . I was furious!

After King's, I went to France to think, and to work out my own vocation. I love broadcasting, and my job now as a radio presenter gives me time to think. I've been to see the vocations people in Westminster, about the possibility of becoming a priest. In the next year I hope to work on spirituality and prayer life, partly at Turvey Abbey which is near here. I feel a sense of vocation, but what's difficult is knowing what it's a vocation to. It might be as a secular priest.

If priesthood were merely a job, nobody would do it. The salary is appalling, so are the perks and the conditions. But it is not just a job, it is about who you are. If God calls you to be a priest you had better get on with it, otherwise you won't be happy. Priesthood can be a hard life, but there is something worse than living a hard life – that is missing your vocation.

For someone like me, a Church which appears to be dominated by a right-wing agenda would seem to be inhospitable. But the Church is roomier than it might appear. It's not 'their' Church to decide who should or should not be part of it. It belongs to all of us.

Of course it is difficult to square being gay with being Catholic. If you believe, as I do, that human sexuality is diverse and God-given, and that homosexuality is merely one variation on it and if you believe that homosexuals can live happily in their relationships, which I do, that would seem to fly in the face of traditional Catholic teaching. No one is more aware of that than me. But Catholic teaching changes although the heart of it does not. What seems to be right, just and overdue, is a Catholic Church able to respond to the value of diverse human sexuality. I'm not saying there should be a free for all, because I'm a firm upholder of sexual morality. But to say that moral sex can only be confined to generative sex between married couples I don't believe is sufficient. Just because it's a difficult subject is no reason not to address it. I do not think the Church has got it right at the moment.

I'll have to think about this very carefully if I am to be a priest. The Church needs to address these questions, to reach those for whom they are matters of life and death, and identity. If the Church is not reaching them it is failing in its mission. To me, being under an obligation of celibacy is not difficult – I am celibate now. I find it a preferable way of living: it makes other things available. It enables me to be much more generous to other people, to be loving in a way that I wasn't before. The main problem is: how do you live with a Catholic teaching which you do not believe in? The answer is through discipline. I try to understand the teaching of the Church and my own position, and to work creatively with the difference between them. In doing that, I am only doing what every other Catholic does, with their sexual problems on contraception, on marriage, etc.

Being a convert helps. No gay friend of mine who was a cradle Catholic is a Catholic now. When you are young, a teenager, coming to terms with your sexuality, the idea of entrusting those problems to a Church which is unsympathetic is very difficult. You need to be older, more experienced, more robust to be able to cope.

The Mass is central to my prayer life and I say morning and evening prayer from the Office every day, which I value enormously. I'd like to get my prayer life more structured, which is why I'm interested in doing some Ignatian spirituality. I pray at my desk in my study. There is a diptych on there, with the very powerful Matisse drawings from the Chapel of the Rosary in Saint Paul de Vence. Sometimes, you get moments when you are just overwhelmed by the presence of God and that can happen in the most unexpected places. It can't be described and it passes understanding.

As I learn more about myself and the Church I've come

to see my Catholicism as something to do with community, understanding yourself as part of this awesome, wonderful creation. And what sustains my faith is the Eucharist, the daily representation of the sacrifice of Christ, where we become what God created us to be. The Church is where the grace of God, the strength, the blessing of God, become available to us all.

It's very hard to be a Christian now, there are so many claims on our allegiances and beliefs. The Church has to go on living the Gospel, proclaiming the Gospel, making the sacraments available. People will always want what the church has to offer and to hear the Gospel. If you do go to church and there is a mechanical Mass, with no joy or liveliness, don't worry, what is important is that you go. It *is* the Mass, even if it's said badly.

The future? In the next 50, 100, 200 years, the Church is going to undergo as radical a change as it ever has. Quite what that will mean I have no idea, but I want to be part of it. The late twentieth century has been a difficult time for the Church, but it has also been exciting. There's lots to be hopeful about. The Church has been around for a long time. Things change but the Church endures.

Polly James

Actress

I have always been a Catholic of sorts. I was educated at Notre Dame Convent in Blackburn and in a sense I was a very religious child because I had to conform to convent living and rules. I spent a lot of time in chapel, singing, learning the Gregorian chant, and at prayer. My imagination is still excited by the religious stories we were brought up with and even if I became the most anti-religious person you could imagine, I could not get rid of those images, particularly the childish stories we were taught, like the birth of Christ and the Three Kings. Christmas is a very emotional time for me, simply because it's imbued with those really mystical stories. Perhaps they also appealed to my sense of drama.

My faith has often helped me. It's where I turn if there's a big problem, not in the sense of, 'Oh God, please let this opening night pass,' though it does make me laugh when I hear everybody on a first night in the theatre saying, 'Oh God, why do we do this, it's so frightening, oh God, please let me get through this.' Total atheists are going around the theatre saying this. We are all calling upon this person that has been there all my life. I suppose in a way I see God as a character, big and friendly.

I do carry a lot of guilt from religion and I did resent

that. We had been brought up in fear and such humility. Of course, you must know when to be humble, but this attitude was at direct odds with getting on in the theatre which required you to say, 'I'm better than anybody and I deserve this part.'

Also we were brought up to fear God, rather than love him. I've had to turn that round somehow in my life, which has left me with this peculiar double set of thinking, looking for the love in religion, rather than the fear. I've had to search out that love because it's not a very happy world and I'm deeply disturbed why God lets it all go on, and nobody's given me an answer.

Religion has played an important part in my life. At a point of crisis in a relationship I was very low and troubled. I felt badness from both of us and realised that it was attacking my very soul. So I took myself to the local priest. He looked about 12 years old and I had come with this very adult problem. I said, 'I'm not sure you're going to be able to help me,' and he said, 'It is a bit out of my depth but I can put you in touch with a convent in Worcester, where I know a nun who has been very helpful to me, she broadcasts a lot, Dame Maria Boulding.'

I went to see her, although she is in an enclosed order. She had that wonderful, pale, opalescent innocence that many nuns have, which leaves you not knowing whether they are 60 or 16. They're timeless. The world's experiences haven't crossed their faces and they're intriguingly beautiful. Yet she knew more about the world and about the difficulties and intimacies of relationships than almost anybody I'd ever come across. Also, because she was completely independent it wasn't like asking a friend. How did she get this wide understanding in an enclosed order?

Simply her spirit and her positive attitude gave me the feeling that I wasn't bad. She made me feel that everybody had the right to be wrong, to make mistakes and to have sinned. Sin for me was always a huge thing that we had to go and tell in confession every Saturday. She gave me a feeling that actually you could resolve these things between yourself and whoever you felt you owed allegiance to. God or whoever. She gave me the feeling that I could carry on.

My relationship with God is very important. I haven't got the brain to get around the great theological questions, but it's important because there has to be a centre. I did have a long period where I went completely against my faith. I didn't do it very overtly, I was far too interested in getting on with working. It simply wasn't there. Then I started asking questions again, and now it's a bit like a full circle and hopefully I'll come back with my personal viewpoint. If you are just given that from the start, how do you know that it's right? I've never had blind faith, and I really envy those who do. Some people seem to have, but then you know how some people walk on stage who seem to have confidence, and they don't.

When it comes to church services I'm not very keen on swinging, guitar-playing rock types. I was brought up with the beautiful sound of the plain chant in my head, so for me the minute I hear that I plug straight back into something that was so comforting for me as a child. It is still comforting.

There's something about me that's always seeking refuge in churches. When I came to London from Blackburn I hadn't a clue that I wouldn't be living in the college, so I went to the YWCA for the first three nights, after which you have to leave. Then I was literally on the streets of London and didn't know what to do. I went to Westminster Cathedral, and I thought the only way to find a priest for certain was to go to confession. At the end I said to the priest, 'I haven't got anywhere to live, I've come to drama school and I've got nowhere to go.' So he took me to the convent nearby, Saint Vincent's, and they took me in for a few weeks until I found a room. So I was living this double life of being a drama student in the swinging sixties by day, and other students saying, 'Where can we rehearse – can we come to your digs?' I would never tell anybody that I was living in a convent.

Being brought up with religion, it's there in you, unless you've stood up and rejected it, and to do that you have to have studied the other side of it. I'm lazy so I've never done that. I call on God when I want to and ignore him when I don't. It's dreadful to say that, but it's true.

I am divorced and all my feelings were against being divorced because I couldn't come to terms with having made my vows in church. How do you get round it? We made our promises in front of our families and friends. I can see that there are situations in marriage, such as great violence, that you have to get out of. I can only say that I would have preferred never to have had to go through it, I can see that it was right, but it is at loggerheads with my inner religious feelings.

I've been lucky because my job has led me to be asked to do all sorts of things. I used to go anywhere to open a fête on a Saturday or Sunday, I adore them. Now it's all changed and fundraising is big, and corporate, and also you find that you spread yourself so thin that you don't exist and you can't do anything well. So over the years I've narrowed it down to two or three things which are very dear to my heart.

One of them is the Hospice movement. They found me, as is nearly always the case, and asked me to be President of a League of Friends at Saint Raphael's Hospice in Cheam, and I think I can honestly say I'd do anything for them because it is one of the most important movements to have come about in the last twenty-five years, because of the breakdown of families. When I was little all my aunties, or great-aunties, became very poorly as they got older, but there was nothing odd about it as we all looked after them. When the final stages of illness would come along, the bed would come downstairs to the front room, and they would have to be looked after during the night. I remember my mum asking me to stay up one night as she was too tired, and it was the first time I saw someone die. It was not terrifying, it was completely natural.

I don't find the idea of death frightening. I lost my brother at a very early age in a road accident and my mother philosophically said a few years later that every family will probably have an incident of that kind on the law of averages. The Hospice movement provides a dignified and even a joyous passage – and that is so valuable.

If I had the opportunity and the right partner I would get married again, but I'd have to get round my previous commitment somehow. I realise that I have made this vow before, and I ask for the chance to make it again.

The nuns at the hospice are such a relief. Many years ago the nuns were very strict with us, but now I find the nuns that run the hospice at St Raphael's such a joy because their lives are truly based in positive love and they seem to have no fear at all. They came to see *A Christmas Carol* I was performing in at the Barbican in London. Ten of them came to the dressing room afterwards, all twittering like little birds, and all the actors came to see them because they could hear this joyous noise coming from my dressing room. I said, 'Does anybody want a glass of Bucks Fizz?' and they refused, then the oldest one said, 'I don't know why you're all saying no, I'm going to say yes.' So immediately all the rest did, and the sight of it! All the actors said the next day, 'We have never seen such beautiful and positive people, having such a joyous reaction,' and the nuns simply said, thank you for your gifts, thank you for giving us your talent. It was very lovely.

John Wilkins

Editor, 'The Tablet'

I would have to go back a bit to explain why I am a Catholic. My parents were both non-conformists, they were Congregationalists and my grandfather had been a Congregationalist minister in New Zealand. He'd gone there because that was mission country. All this meant that I didn't know any Catholics. Even when I was at university, I hardly knew they existed. However, my mother became rather High Anglican. She was not interested in doctrine or anything like that but as she was half Welsh, she liked the hymns. My father became agnostic but never atheist. I was with him about an hour before he died and it was clear that he had a residual confidence in the life to come. Some sort of faith was pulling him up.

I was brought up in the Anglican ethos which I respected and I thought the values were good. Then when I was at Cambridge University, there was a period when I realised that although I valued the religion I had been taught, it was only my mother's religion and I had no real reason to believe it myself. So I had a short period when I experienced unbelief and it became clear to me that if you do not believe in God you act differently.

I had been at Cambridge two years studying classics and

I strayed into the church of St Mary Redcliffe in Bristol for Evensong one Sunday. Evensong is arguably the most beautiful service that Anglicans have, and I had some sort of religious experience, the only one I have, had in my life. It was impossible to describe, rather like a love affair. It is something that does not have meaning for other people because it's only for you. It might have something to do with the fact that I was in love at the time. If you are loved humanly, you understand about this other sort of love. For some time I felt as though I had another existence, lifted right out of the normal level into another level. That was an extraordinary experience and there was a great deal of awe in it. I was quite frightened because I felt that I had come into contact with a force that I did not understand. It was a calling. So I stopped reading classics and read theology and philosophy, and I had very good teachers.

One was Bishop John Robinson, who wrote *Honest To God*; he was the Dean of my college. Another man I am greatly indebted to is an Evangelical, Canon Charlie Moule, and I also came into contact with the great Donald McKinnon who was an extraordinary person. He really showed me what philosophy could be. Whereas other people would read from their textbook, he would actually think in front of you. Sometimes it would be a disaster and he would say, 'I'm afraid this has been a most terrible lecture, I will try and do better next time.'

I gradually became aware that somewhere in all this there was a hole in the middle of everything I was learning. It didn't measure up to the religious experience I'd had. At first I couldn't think what it was, but something was missing.

One Christmas I found myself in Westminster Cathedral. You can never say whether these things are chance or not. An extraordinary sort of theatre was going on inside and I was spellbound by this. I had never seen anything like it. At the end of the Mass I was probably a Catholic by desire.

I would never say that the Eucharist in the Church of England doesn't have an effect because many Anglican friends are nourished on that, but it didn't nourish me. Eucharist was rather for special people who were with a capital 'R' religious. But my experience in the Cathedral gave me this feeling that religion really is here, not up there somewhere, it is operating in the middle of everything. Eventually, I came to the conclusion the Catholic Church was for me.

This was all during the sixties at the time of the Second Vatican Council. I saw the revolution produced by that council which really had started at the roots of the Church, among the faithful. In the Catholic Church change and development always seem to come from the roots.

Unlike many people becoming Catholics now, what was not important to me was authority. Actually, I have always had difficulties with Catholic authority and I don't like the way that authority is exercised inside the Church at the moment. But at that Mass it became clear to me that in fact this radical thing that could produce a revolution goes back almost like an umbilical cord to the Upper Room and the Last Supper. This was what I had been looking for to fill this hole.

All these things just came together. I don't use the word conversion because conversion is when you really change – stop going along one road and go along another. I have never turned my back on anything in my Anglican heritage, I have just gone on the same road but quite a long way further forward.

I was received into the Catholic Church in 1965, the closing year of the Second Vatican Council. At that time I was working for *Frontier,* an ecumenical Anglican paper. One of my colleagues asked, 'Was it the mystical side of the Catholic church that drew you?' and I was rather interested in this, as this man was a well-known Evangelical layman.

It was as though he felt there was a mystical dimension missing in his church. My mother was very surprised about my decision. She said, 'If I had brought John up properly, I am sure it would never have happened.'

One friend who was studying theology said, 'This is the end of our friendship, I couldn't possibly be associated with someone like yourself who has become a Catholic.' Most of my friends, though, accepted it. Another said, 'John doesn't normally make these bold decisions.' I think his observation was right. It didn't seem to me such a sharp change though. I just slipped into the Catholic Church quietly one day and I have never, in spite of everything, looked back.

Yet at the moment, I do not think I would become a Catholic. It doesn't mean to say I think I made a mistake, but the church of John Paul II would not have attracted me in the same way. The revolution of Vatican Two which inspired me has lost its impetus, particularly the idea that the Church would be governed in a collegial way.

I remember the late Bishop Christopher Butler saying to me, 'There is a moral obligation for the Pope now to govern collegially', but he doesn't need to. What Pope John Paul means when he uses the word 'collegiality' is a team following the captain. Although Vatican II emphasised the importance of the team, the Pope seems to mean that you are being collegial as a team member if you agree with him.

I think that the Catholic Church is the wickedest church but it's also by far the holiest and what matters at the end of the day, in Christian life, is love and I do think that you're nearer the heart of that love in the Catholic Church, and it's a passionate love.

It is often said that to become a Catholic in England you have to have two conversions – one to the Catholic faith and the other to the Catholic community, I never found that. In the Catholic Church you meet all classes and become immediately at home, part of the whole community.

My main temptation is despair. Usually it's very hard to know what our worst sins are. But mine is a total despair of life and existence and the worth of living. Usually I am a very buoyant person but sometimes these black clouds used to simply descend on me. I go birdwatching in Sheppey in the Thames. One day I had one of these black clouds when the sense of failure was on me and I sat on a log beside the water. The woman who was with me never said anything, just stared. The sun was on the waves and wading birds were flying in packs, all turning at once. I thought, 'It is all worth it', and I have never again ever had that black cloud. Now it is the Catholic Church, particularly with its confession routine and forgiveness, and the feeling that the Communion of Saints is very near that keeps that despair out. The real joy in life is that you can wake up in the morning and you can think it's wonderful to be a Catholic. Although I do find it much harder being a Catholic in the Church of Pope John Paul II than I did under John XXIII, it's a real test of my faith, I am aware that the present Pope has got something to do with that feeling when I wake up.

I would like to see the Church change greatly. The late Peter Hebblethwaite wrote a book called *The Runaway Church* at the time of Paul VI; well, the Catholic Church is not a runaway church and some one was bound to rein it back as the present Pope has done but now it has become like a boiling kettle with the lid on. One change I think is needed fairly quickly is for the Church to have a married priesthood as well as a celibate priesthood in the secular clergy and I expect that to come very fast, perhaps in my lifetime. That's particular important in Latin America where there has been the biggest loss of ground to the Catholic Church since the Reformation. Evangelicals have made enormous headway there because of this lack of priests. We cannot go on putting the celibacy of the priesthood before providing the Eucharist for the faithful. Religious orders would always have their celibate priests, so celibacy would not disappear and I am a great believer in chosen celibacy.

We also need a pluralistic Church where bishops are not civil servants working for the main management. The Church is not an army marching to the orders of a general, it's a communion. That means that bishops' conferences in each country must be allowed to have their head.

It's always said that Popes alternate. After a very strong centralising Pope like the present one, we need a man who puts the emphasis on the team and not on the captain.

I also think the Church must update its teaching on sex. There is now a chasm you can't cross between what the Church teaches and many of the people. As far as the Church is concerned, it's as though the social sciences didn't exist.

Prayer is important to me and I like to pray through the Mass. Sometimes I also pray when I am driving along. I repeat the Jesus Prayer or the Our Father and the Hail Mary, sort of arrow prayers. There is a saying that a short prayer goes quickest. I do find it difficult to have time for more set prayer, particularly in the evenings. One of the things that helped me here was the Jesuit William T. Johnston. He has this prayer where you simply repeat the name of the Lord. So you say 'Jesus, Jesus, Jesus' and that concentrates your mind. You go on saying that and it should go off into silence at a certain point. I have tried that a lot and found it very good because it stops those distractions to which we are all so prone. The other thing is Ignatian prayer, where you fasten on to things in the world, seeing God in every one of them. For me, with my particular job, and my particular interests, and particular character, that's good.

In spite of my disappointments with the present Church, I have no regrets about becoming a Catholic. Even at the time of *Humanae Vitae*, Pope Paul VI's encyclical on human life, which was a terrific blow because it was the beginning of stopping change and development in the Church, I was not sorry. I still kept to that thing which brought me into the Church, my trust in it. For example, some of the great theologians of Vatican II were in disgrace shortly before. Teilhard de Chardin, who is a great spiritual teacher for today, was also under a cloud. People like me have suffered quite a lot during the last years. We have seen so many things we believed in sidelined, but my faith has not been damaged because there is a truth in the Church which is fundamental, and it holds you.

John Patten

Former Secretary of State

I am a cradle Catholic, My mother was Austrian. She came to England in the late 1920s to marry my father who was English and at least nominally Anglican. I was brought up as Catholic and educated by the nuns and by the Jesuits.

My first school was Saint Peter's Primary School which is still Roman Catholic. Then I went to Wimbledon College which was a Jesuit grammar school and is now comprehensive. So I had nuns with rulers followed by Jesuits with ferulas. However, this kind of treatment did not put me off the Church because I'm a very straightforward, orderly sort of fellow and I always really rather liked religion. It puts things clearly; good is good, and bad is bad, and God is there as a sort of eternal referee to make sure you're on the right side of the divide. I also like the concept of a religion that knows what it stands for. In fact, Saint Ignatius of Loyola is my favourite saint because he was tough.

My father subcontracted the whole business of my religious education to my mother and I think he approved of the fact that the nuns with their rulers and the Jesuits with their ferulas generally kept order and educated me in a robust sort of way where good manners were part of life. That's why so many Protestants, and even some agnostics and atheists want to send their children to Roman Catholic schools these days.

My mother used to go to church with her Latin missal and her German translation, dodging between the two. When we got English in the Mass it made things terribly confusing. She would have three books on her knees at various stages. She just assumed I would go to church and I just went. My daughter, who's eight, is being brought up in the same sort of way, she's at a very good Roman Catholic primary school where they give her a very free and easy education. But it is also rather tough, learning tables and spelling, rather old fashioned things disapproved of by the chattering classes these days. So far she seems to have taken to it like a duck to water.

I never had any doubts about my faith even when I was growing up. Whether that's through intellectual laziness or I missed out some vital stage in my life I don't know. I have never experienced any 'dark nights of the soul'. Happily my wife, who is also a Catholic, feels exactly the same way.

I have old-fashioned views and I believe in the teaching of the Church, the papacy, and all that. I'm rather like Monsignor Alfred Gilbey who is a very old friend of ours. He married us in 1978 when I was an undergraduate at Cambridge and he was the Roman Catholic chaplain. In answer to the question; 'What do you think of women priests?' He is quoted as saying; 'If it's all right by the Pope, it's all right by me'. And that's basically my view.

I like the Roman Catholic religion because it gives moral certainties, which I happen to believe. Being a Catholic helps in ministerial life as it should do in professional or business life because you should always have a touchstone of what is right and wrong. I often talk to Chris Patten, the Governor of Hong Kong (no relation), about these matters too. He's also a Roman Catholic, I'm godfather to his daughter and he's godfather to mine. He was best man at our wedding, and we've been friends for twenty-five years.

Unless you have certainties in things being right or wrong you get into terrible trouble. We live in such a relativist age with such a reductionist attitude to everything. Some time ago my wife Louise and I sat either side of a bishop, not a Catholic, at a dinner in Oxford. First she, and then I, tried to get out of him, whether he though abortion was right or wrong. We simply could not get him to say yes or no. So, in a very gentle way we gave up.

There are eight core-values I would like to see promoted, especially among children. In fact, I think they are essential for all of society. They are: acceptance of personal responsibility, respect for authority, self-reliance, discipline, unselfishness and self-restraint, honesty and trustworthiness, loyalty and fidelity and, finally, courtesy.

I must say that today I am more hopeful that we can bring back these values. It is becoming more 'politically correct' for people to talk about right and wrong. Moral issues are discussed in the House far more now than they ever were. Things are changing. For example, even as recently as the 1980s you had to be reasonably brave to stand up for pro-life issues. That is no longer the case. The party to which I belong still respects freedom of conscience, which means that I have always been able to vote against such things as abortion, hanging or euthanasia. In fact, it is no longer difficult to be a Catholic in the House of Commons. When I first came here there were certain suspicions about Catholics, but now we have all 'outed' ourselves and if you are a Catholic you are known as one.

I say my prayers morning and evening and go to Mass on Sundays to honour the obligation. I don't become involved in the prayer groups in the Commons, but I have been to the occasional Roman Catholic Mass here. It is celebrated by our chaplain, Father Seed, who is the Cardinal's secret weapon for bringing in the likes of innocent Anglicans and others to the Roman Catholic Church.

When we're in London, as a family, we go regularly to Westminster Cathedral because it's next door, but our main parish is the Church of Saint Peter in Eynsham in West Oxfordshire. There we have had, until very recently, Father Tolkien, who is the eldest son of J. R. R. Tolkien, and who is 76 and living in retirement in North Oxford. He was extremely holy. My daughter was devoted to him. When we started taking her to church at about two or three, like all little girls she wriggled and caused trouble, but then she fell for Father Tolkien and they developed a new liturgical act: at the end of Mass she would run across the church and leap into his arms as he came out of the sacristy; she was devoted to him. Now we have a very good man, Father Mead, who has just retired from being an army chaplain for nineteen years. My wife is a reader, and my daughter likes joining in things. She quite often takes up the Communion wine at the offertory and so on. On Christmas Eve, as the youngest child in the church she carried the baby Jesus up to the crib, so we do get involved and we have some good friends there.

I've found the clearest spiritual guidance in recent years, coming from the last Chief Rabbi, Dr Jacobovitz and from the present Chief Rabbi, Jonathan Sacks, who is a friend. I freely admit to being under the spell of both of them. Jonathan Sacks has a very clear mind and he is able to express things in a very clear way. There is a passage in one of his books, I am paraphrasing it but not parodying it, where he says; we give children condoms but we don't give them a sense of value. He has a straightforward, non-relativist philosophy. These two rabbis are fearless about speaking out and they don't mind upsetting people. Because of this, the Jews do seem to have a disproportionate influence in public life.

I'd like to see Catholics developing their voice and having more of a network to help them do this. I like the way my Jewish friends put their families first. When I've been to dinner with them, or joined them in celebrating Jewish festivals in their homes, there is an intense sense of family pride and togetherness. One thing we've learnt from our Jewish friends is the importance of families eating together.

The result is that in our own home we do try to sit around the table, with our tiny family, Louise, Mary Claire, me and our two Burmese cats, and we sit and talk as much as we can.

When I was a junior minister in Northern Ireland I was regarded as a 'castle Catholic' in the neo-colonial terminology,' I was a Catholic and I was 'up at the castle' in the same way as in the Indian empire there were certain Indians who would throw themselves into the area of colonial administrators and be almost part of their world. One thing that really got up and smacked me in the face was a Saint Patrick's night dinner run by the Catholic group, the Knights of Saint Columba. I was taken round to be introduced to all sorts of people. There was a bishop there and he said, 'Come and meet this chap, he's a retired leader of the IRA. Of course he's the old-fashioned sort, he'd only ever shoot soldiers or policemen, never civilians. He's one of the better sort.' I gulped. But I was learning.

Before I went to Northern Ireland I saw myself as a Catholic Unionist, and I remain one since I believe you can't expel a part of the United Kingdom, however inconvenient. None of my experiences there taught me that it was right to expel the people of the Province from the United Kingdom. There are lots of inconvenient parts of Britain, Toxteth, or Tower Hamlets, for example, but we don't try to get rid of them. But being in Ireland didn't have any great spiritual effect on me, though when I was there I witnessed the world speed record for saying Mass. We used to go outside Hillsborough to some place in the country that was judged to be safe. It was a church nicknamed 'Riley's Trench' and we heard Mass there in nineteen minutes flat, which is pretty good going

I always wanted to be a don, and when I was very young I was elected to a job at Oxford, and I was a Fellow of the College. I was given forty-three years tenure. It was on a little slip of paper saying that I would retire on December 30th, 2013. It was rather like going into a Turkish jail to do a forty-three-year sentence and given your release date on a slip of paper. But there's no remission for good conduct. Academic life can be entrancing in some ways, but I found the politics of an Oxford senior college rather nasty sometimes, far nastier than in the Commons. Here it's perfectly charming; you can have a knockabout in the Chamber and then go and have a cup of tea and talk, or a glass of beer as I sometimes do with my Labour Party friends afterwards.

I got drawn into party politics by a set of accidents and being in the right place at the right time. Having been a councillor in Oxford, and a seat becoming vacant, I fought it, being told we probably wouldn't get it, but we did in 1979 and we've been there ever since. I find trying to help my constituents very interesting, and I'm not quite sure if it's meant to be rewarding. It's not totally and there were a number of things that I set out to try to do, but you'll have to wait until my memoirs are published posthumously before you know what they were.

A friend of mine, credited with changing Lady Thatcher's voice, Sir Gordon Reece, a Roman Catholic, a very good man, always sends his friends books at Christmas. This year he sent me two, a kind of lighthearted one, and a Benedictine prayer book, which is pretty fierce and has morning and evening prayers for each day of the week. At the bottom of each page there is a terrifying little sentence like 'Don't eat and sleep too much' or, 'If you face temptation, throw yourself against Christ'. One I find especially helpful is, 'Each day we begin again.'

I've read the Gospels several times around, I try to read a chapter every day. I am also kept on the straight and narrow by my private secretary, Elizabeth Fleming, who is my strong right arm. She is a severe Roman Catholic and a Eucharistic minister. I'm never let off the leash by her,

It's easier to keep on the straight and narrow when you're older, it's much more difficult when you're a teenager. Nowadays, people tend to condemn the 1960s but I always draw back from such criticism. I had a very nice time then and I hope no one else finds out.

Moira Lister

Actress

I remember my mother saying, Never discuss politics or religion!' Both subjects are bound to raise the blood-pressure, and being a fighting Irish spirit, she knew what she was talking about. Religion was not taken lightly in our family. They were strongly Catholic, with several nuns and priests to their credit, and my religion has always been an enormous help.

My parents went to South Africa just before I was born, my two sisters having been born in Scotland, so I was dubbed the only 'Zulu' in the family. I was sent to a strict convent school in Johannesburg, and when I left Africa for England and the stage at 18, alone and in the middle of the Battle of the Atlantic, my religious upbringing was so strong that I simply put myself in Our Lady's hands and she took over my life. All things that were right for me, she gave me. Other things for which I prayed, but she didn't consider appropriate, she did not.

Looking back on those early days I was blessed to have such blind faith. Of course, during the tough times, of which I have had my share, I have questioned my beliefs, but every time I start to doubt, some guiding light seems to say to me, 'Remember you were born with the gift of faith.' I have come to realise that I cannot live without believing that there is a Supreme Presence that has conceived and created our planet. It is impossible that it all just happened. It is too perfect. Of course no one has come up with the definite answer as to how it came about. That is a measure of the brilliance of the plan, that absolutely nobody has managed to 'crack it'. A lot of theories claim to have found the answers, but not even the ones who have 'gone aloft' have been able to come back and tell us. So the mystery remains. And all we are left with is our own belief.

Strange, inexplicable things have happened in my life. For some unknown reason, out in Africa, I had a devotion to our Lady of Lourdes, even though I didn't know where Lourdes was! Yet, when I came to marriageable age, she found for me a 'local boy' in the form of Vicomte d'Orthez. The town of Orthez is thirty kilometres from Lourdes, and it was on my husband's grandfather's estate that Bernadette had her vision of Mary. The Church offered the grandfather a royalty on every rosary sold in exchange for land on which to build a basilica. He, of course, refused to accept a penny but gave the land outright to the Church. That was why my husband Jacques had the nickname 'Lucky d'Orthez', because he said he had a huge bank account in Heaven. And I benefited from that bonus because we were married for forty wonderful years.

Sadly, his luck ran out at the end because he suffered a terrible stroke and was unable to speak for four years. But in a paradoxical way we grew even closer during the time that I nursed him, and I know our prayers gave us the strength to get through, and even more so after he died and I developed a life-threatening cancer, which I survived.

As a sort of thanksgiving I decided to go to the shrine of Medjugorie in the former Yugoslavia. It is said that, once you go there, your life changes. Mine certainly has. It was quite a hairy experience, getting there. Landing in

Zagreb in the middle of the war, on to Split, then a 120-mile taxi drive into the mountains, past check-points with sten-guns pointed in our faces – useful hostages we could be – through desolate villages, bypassing Mostar just twenty miles away which had been decimated, but still the sound of gunfire whistling through the night. Eventually we came to this oasis of prayer and faith. It is said they tried to bomb Medjugorie but the valley filled with cloud and the pilots were enshrouded and had to turn back.

Medjugorie is a place where faith is tangible. It is dedicated to the pursuit of peace. It is totally simple and rustic, with only one small hotel and one huge modern church, where wonderful priests of every nationality take time to listen and guide and give all the spiritual help you need.

Behind the church is a high mountain which is very steep and rocky and at intervals all the way up are Stations of the Cross. At the top is a sea of crosses of every shape and size which pilgrims have carried up and planted there. It is awe-inspiring.

In the chapel of Perpetual Adoration I had a strange experience. I was alone in the chapel praying, when suddenly I felt that every cell in my body had been given a Vitamin B12 injection. I didn't see anything, but what I felt took my breath away. And since that time I seem to be living a charmed life – long may it last!

Maybe because my faith is so important to me, and I care so much about the Church, I feel there are several things that need to be done in our churches. First I would like to suggest that there should be a school for preachers, they could learn so much from actors. Often I find myself thinking about my Sunday lunch rather than the saving of my soul, simply because the microphone is not properly tested and adjusted and secondly because the content of the sermons, excellent as it may be, is presented in a droning and boring way instead of 'performed' to have the greatest possible impact on the congregation, which surely is the point of it.

Also, I deplore the lack of respect in churches. Ushers and ministers of the Eucharist in jeans or open-necked shirts. Where are the altar boys and the surplices they used to wear? What has happened to Sunday Schools?

Other bones of contention for me are the Church rules on contraception. Surely some middle course could be found, if only to save the appalling suffering of the unwanted children.

And on another note, could the priests come to visit their parishioners more often? I find two visits in forty years a little less than adequate. When I was young, the visit of the priest was part of our upbringing. And why have I never seen a Catholic priest backstage? They could do so much good.

I would like to share what I think is a heartwarming story about a priest. Years ago I was going through a harrowing time, as we all do at some stage in our lives, and I happened to go to Mass in the country, in the back room of a pub. The priest, although badly in need of some new vestments, to say nothing of new shoes, gave a sermon which lifted me out of my torpor to such an extent, that I felt that I must talk to him because he was the closest I have ever been to a real saint. After Mass we spent a completely healing hour together and all my pain disappeared. I had to leave the next day for Africa. When I got there, I sent him a 'thank you' letter which included a cheque which I though he sorely needed. Some weeks later, the cheque was returned with my signature torn off it, and a little note saying he couldn't possibly accept the money but he hoped I wouldn't object that as his housekeeper was a fan of mine he had given her my signature to stick in her autograph book.

Clifford Longley

Religious journalist

I am a Catholic because I couldn't be anything else. None of the alternatives is better, because Catholicism is true. Do I regret becoming a Catholic as I did thirty-four years ago? Do I want to go somewhere else? No.

I am very comfortable in the Catholic Church and have a strong sense that is where I ought to be and where I am at home. This makes me infinitely more capable of putting up with the nonsense that sometimes goes on in Catholicism. None of it, however, begins to call into question whether I'm in the right place. It's like a nationality or an identity. One's identity is set, it's fixed. You're English – let's take that as an analogy. I can't stand John Major but it doesn't stop me being English, or mean I'm going to emigrate to Spain. It's the same with the Catholic Church. Of course it can be very uncomfortable and disturbing but it's familiar, the right place to be and there's a tremendous richness, diversity and ordinariness about Catholics which makes them very good company.

I remember being attracted to the intellectual rigour of Catholicism as a philosophical system that stood on its own feet and thought it could prove itself to the first principles and did a reasonably good job of it. It had centuries of high-quality debate in its tradition and experience, to which one could relate, read about and adopt oneself and I hadn't found that in my experiences, slim though they may have been, of the alternatives. Anglicans or Protestants did not seem to me to have the same degree of intellectual rigour.

I had Catholic friends at university and eventually asked one what do I do about becoming a Catholic. He said go and see the chaplain. I knocked on the presbytery door and the Irish housekeeper appeared and asked me what I wanted. I just blurted out that I wanted to talk to the priest about becoming a Catholic. 'Oh,' she said, 'he's away. Come back next month.' That seemed to me a marvellous statement of the self-confidence of the Catholic Church, which earned my instant respect. Had she said, 'Oh, come in, we'll pray over you. What a tremendous favour you are doing us', I would perhaps in the short term have been more captivated but in the long term not have been held so securely.

This rather indifferent brush-off was exactly the right reply and this is very much in line with the rule of Saint Benedict, I have since discovered. When a young monk presents himself to the abbot and asks to be admitted to the community, he must above all not be welcomed and must be held at a distance. They knew what they doing. They had a confidence that if you want to do something seriously, that will not put you off. Since then I have taken the view that when from time to time one is in conversation with people who want to become Catholics, one can probably be quite helpful by trying to talk them out of it. One shouldn't minimise the difficulties, so that if they do go ahead they know what they are doing.

I had been much influenced in my search by a former Anglican clergyman at Oxford. He'd become a Catholic in the pre-Vatican era and had followed the route taken by many before, as charted by Cardinal Newman. Many of the books he lent me by Newman were not in defence of Catholicism, but in defence of truth and dogma. This was a very enlightened kind of Catholicism. It wasn't the Catholicism of *Brideshead Revisited*, or Vatican I, or the average Irish parish. In fact it was the Catholicism that began to come to birth after the Second Vatican Council. So in a sense I joined the Second Vatican Council Church even though the Council had not even been convened at that point.

My biggest difficulty, frankly – it sounds absurd to say it now – was whether God existed at all. To be trite about it: if God exists the rest is easy, including being a Catholic. The existence of God did remain an intellectual difficulty even as I approached my baptism. As I had been brought up an atheist, so had not been baptised before, I had the privilege of being baptised in adulthood. I approached my baptism with this one reservation: if there is a God then everything I am doing is fine and I am comfortable with it. But I was still not quite sure.

Then I had a most extraordinary experience. I went to spend a weekend at Quarr Abbey in the Isle of Wight, just to reflect and think. I remember sitting in a garden and thinking, what I am about to do is absolutely absurd. There's obviously no God – the non-existence of God is self-evident – how on earth could I ever have persuaded myself otherwise. My parents were atheists and atheism had been the intellectual world I'd inhabited until that moment, and it still seemed at that moment completely convincing and all the alternatives preposterous. I said to myself, this is terribly embarrassing, obviously the whole thing has gone completely dry on me and evaporated. I've no problems about the Catholic bit and all the sacraments and so on – the existence of God is the problem.

I thought probably the best thing to do in order not to disappoint people and make a complete idiot of myself, was to go through with the baptism. I could always quietly drop it after that. I didn't want to make a great fuss and have a big quarrel with people because 'sorry, I've decided God doesn't exist.' So I kept the appointment and turned up at the font and had this really rather embarrassing ceremony, because clearly it was an adapted version of what they do for children. I had sponsors, a couple of blokes on my course who came along rather sheepishly and I felt intensely self-conscious about the whole thing, rather wishing I was somewhere else. But the extraordinary thing is that the baptism obviously 'took' because I have never once been able recapture that experience that I had in the garden in Quarr Abbey. It is almost as if I don't know how to recapture it. It was rather like crossing a bridge and then blowing the bridge up. I don't know why. You might say it was the grace of the sacrament of baptism, but certainly a switch was thrown which can't be thrown back again.

During the ceremony I felt quite dissociated from it all, rather cold and embarrassed about the whole thing. We all know that sometimes you go to Mass and it 'takes' and you feel terribly captured in it and sometimes you go and you aren't quite sure you're even there.

One of the big changes that becoming a Catholic made to me was that it imposed an answerableness . . . a having to answer to another, existing completely independently of me. Before I had been answerable only to myself, because in the atheist world there is only oneself.

This realisation had fundamental importance in who I was or who I wanted to become. My definition of humanity changed and so did my ideals and values. Also I recognised the limitations of rationality and that the clever, intellectual, logical, rational analysis can only lead at most, half way to the truth. There was a need for another level of truth than that including the moral. As an atheist I'd been a rationalist and I had regarded logical truth as being the only test, but now I realised that there were other tests.

Although the Catholic church is a home in which I feel

entirely comfortable, it can be uncomfortable and even disturbing. And, of course, like any other organisation run by human beings, it could be better.

The Vatican, for example, could be dismantled and replaced by a slimmer and less authoritarian institution. I do think it is the institution, not individuals that is at fault. I like the notion of subsidiarity and would like the bishops' conferences to have a few years expanding their scope and seeing how they get on. They could develop their bilateral relationships and loosen their unilateral bonds to the centre in Rome.

The history of the Church has been a series of zig-zags. We zigged one way with John XXIII and we are zagging another way with John Paul II. I have felt embarrassed by the present Pope in the past and may well feel embarrassed by him in the future. I am ashamed of his hard line on contraception: of the way he handled the Buddhists in his book; of the concept of a 'mega-pope' with his popular cult. I am embarrassed when the Church gets things wrong and I am mortified when it gets things very wrong. We need to return to a post-conciliar model of the Church. It is a simple fact that the reform of the church which Vatican II proposed had not got far when the cardinals met in 1978 in a state of fear and trembling to elect a new pope because their first choice Pope John Paul had died. And they rushed over to a totally different option.

If I were Pope, the first thing I would do would be to recognise and appreciate the value of bishops' conferences. Bishops are an essential part of the Church and they should be encouraged to develop the maximum openness with two-way communications between themselves, their priests and the laity. They would oversee the work of the theologians in their dioceses, deal with local administration, laicisation of priests and the general exposition of doctrine. The Pope would have an over-sight of what was going on, but would not try to run the whole thing from the centre.

While the relationship between clergy and laity should change, it should not be dramatic or revolutionary. I think a change in the theology of the laity is due; the Pope himself has encouraged this in his writings. I would like that to be carried through in action and the laity given their proper importance. If taken seriously, that would mean, for instance, that we would have synods, not just of bishops, but synods of bishops, clergy and laity. What I mean is, in deciding where the Church should go from here, we should hear many voices and not just the voice of bishops. The more the bishops listen to the clergy and laity at local level, the better they will listen at international level.

Ultimately, the Papacy is a good idea; authority residing in one person makes sense in an incarnational religion. Similarly, it is important that there be a central core of moral teaching, but there should be a more pastoral and perhaps less rigid way of applying the doctrines to particular cases. But at the moment there is a vast accretion to the Papacy of extraneous power that ought not to belong to it. Some appalling mistakes have been made and responsibility must be taken for them. And in so far as those mistakes may have produced contemporary consequences, we have to try to correct them.

People in the Church whom I admire greatly include John Henry Newman; his English style, his intellectual integrity and intellectual restlessness; his impatience with second best (for him). I can relate to him and sympathise with him. I also admire Cardinal Hume. He has a peculiar combination of firmness and sweetness which I suppose comes from being a combination of English gentleman, monk and possibly saint, I don't know. He has done wonders for the Catholic Church here and often he has done that by saying or doing nothing other than by being there. And maybe that's a lesson the Pope needs to learn.

I am quite ready to accept the Church's self-definition as the community Christ founded on the Apostles and that its history can be traced straight back to the original. That seems to me to authenticate it. I am quite happy therefore to journey on in this ancient and rather rusty old ship.

Delia Smith

Cookery writer and BBC presenter

I became a Catholic when I was twenty-two because I suppose I fell in love. It was love for the Church and especially for the Mass. My first visit to a Mass drew me to the Church even though I didn't know what was going on because it was all in Latin. But there was something so human and tangible about it and also something deeply mysterious. It was, and still is, wonderful and I try and go every day. The whole sacramental system of the Church is a great help to me and my prayer life.

I had a varied religious upbringing. My parents weren't religious in any formal sense but my mother taught me to pray regularly. I remember her showing me a picture of Jesus as the Good Shepherd, with children around him, and saying that I was praying to him. I went to every kind of Church – a Methodist Sunday school, Congregationalist Brownies and Church of England youth group – but nothing really gelled, much as I wanted to belong to a church.

During my school years at Bexley in Kent I was brought up as a Christian and had regular scripture lessons. As I was good at reading, though I must say at not much else, I was always asked to read in RE lessons and various ceremonies like carol services. I loved all the stories from the

Bible. I suppose gradually the message was also becoming important to me.

Then I had a boyfriend who was Catholic. Once he was giving me a lift home and he asked me to get something from the glove compartment of his car. Inside I saw a book that looked like a Bible and he told me it was a missal and that he was a Roman Catholic. I remember my heart sinking and thought: 'Catholic, they're people who have lots of children to get more Catholics.' Until then I had never met a Catholic.

I soon realised that his religion was very important to him. For example, he never missed Mass, and I was quite impressed by that and also that he wasn't what you'd call a 'holy type', and he had plenty of girlfriends.

One Sunday I went with him to Mass. It was all in Latin and I didn't understand a word, but something drew me to it and I started going regularly on my own. I liked the way that people dressed so casually even in jeans. It seemed so human compared with the way I had been brought up to think you had to dress up to go to church. Then some Catholic friends gave me the autobiography of St Thérèse of Liseux. Even though it was very difficult to read I just knew that there was something of the truth about God in it. I don't know how we recognise the truth but I thought, 'This is it, she's got it.' This is what I think God is like too.

Then I started thinking about becoming a Catholic and was drawn into Catholic circles. I got more and more into St Thérèse's spirituality and I went on a pilgrimage to Liseux with Mgr Vernon Johnson.

At that time I disagreed with nothing about the Church. As I said, I became a convert because I fell in love in a way, and a person who falls in love doesn't see any faults. I was starry eyed about it all. But gradually over the years I began to see how wrong some of it was.

Of course you have got to have leadership and structure, but I think the whole thing has gone way off, and needs updating. Sometimes the Church doesn't seem to be talking about the same God that I have come to know. I was received into the Church during Vatican II, but it's so different now; there is understanding and compassion but the official hard line is beyond what some people can manage to follow. Nevertheless, a sincere person who is seeking the truth will never be denied it.

I am still happy to stay a Catholic but I do think that the Church must evolve. We are moving towards a new era and the Church must move too. As I said, the Mass is most important to me and I believe it should be celebrated in every church daily, but in so many places now there are simply not enough priests. What are we going to do about that? It seems wrong that we expect priests to be one-man bands who have to fill far too many roles – counsellor, social worker, administrator, accountant, always on call to anyone. It's too much strain to put on one person. Although I think priests should be able to choose if they marry or not, I do not think that marriage would necessarily solve this, because the great workload they carry would also put a huge strain on a marriage as it often does in the Church of England, where many clergy marriages collapse. One thing that the Catholic priest does *not* have is the worry of a wife and children. What I would like to see is shared ministry, with members of the community exercising their different gifts, such as preaching and counselling. Within that shared ministry someone would be responsible for the liturgy. Maybe that person would be called a priest but the role would be different; for instance, they might not be the preacher, or hear confessions.

One important change I would like to see in the Church's official teaching is a greater emphasis on compassion rather than authority and condemnation. It is there, but not enough. The Church sets standards too high for us to follow. I feel that much of the teaching on marriage, on homosexuality, for example, is just too hard. I am particularly upset by the Church's attitude towards homosexuality. It seems to me to go against all I believe about God. Of course the Church must say what is right and what is wrong but God made all people different. It is no good saying 'That may be how God made you, but that is not the way you are supposed to be.' It is a very complicated area, but I do think there has to be some change in understanding and attitude.

Among those who have influenced my spiritual life are St Thérèse, Ruth Burroughs, the Prioress of the Carmelite convent in Norwich and Sister Wendy Beckett, who has become a great friend.

I am happy in the Catholic Church, even with all its failings. This is not to say I am exclusivist. I went to a wonderful Presbyterian Holy Week service in Belfast, and to a tremendous service for people with AIDS held in the Anglican church of Saint-Martin-in-the-Fields, which, as well as Christians, was attended by Muslims and Jews as well. When I go to services such as these I find myself feeling that we are moving towards a world religion.

Prayer is crucial to my daily life and I believe that all we have to do to pray is to make space and time. Prayer is not something we do; it is something God does if we allow him to. I try to give him between half and three-quarters of an hour each day. If you include the Mass, it is more and the best time of the day for me is early in the morning. I find it hard to use the word prayer to 'lift my mind and heart to God', as the Catechism said. My mind races around so. But what I have learned from Thérèse and from Rachel and Sister Wendy is that it is the actual wanting to give the time and space to God that is the important thing. So I just leave it to God and he takes care of it. Most of the time I don't feel anything, no nice religious feelings, no cosiness, no sense that I am 'giving God His due'. Maybe that is what the Gospels mean when they talk about poverty of spirit, and I am sure that everybody has a relationship with God whether they know it or not.

I don't think I'm very good at prayer. I feel it's a bit like my jam making. If I took my jam to a WI it wouldn't win. Imagine a father working in his study and his two-year-old daughter coming in while he is working: she is playing, running around and all kinds of things. The important thing is that she has come into his study to be with him. She can't be on his level, but she is saying, 'I want to be with you.' That's how I feel about my relationship with God. Going to Mass is a tangible way of saying that I want to be with God. At Mass I hear Scripture. I remember St Thérèse saying that the Gospels never lose their freshness. I can't say I feel that, though sometimes a line does speak to me in a special way. When I told Sister Wendy I did not often feel inspired by Scripture, she said that St Thérèse died when she was only 24. I'm now 54.

I do find that the healthiest position to be in my prayer life is to have nothing and this is very difficult for some people. They want to have nice prayer feelings for God. I know some people who would go so far as not going to work because they have faith that God will provide for them. That's not for me. Faith for me is about being poor, not feeling that I am giving God His due, doing what I am supposed to do.

The Catholic Church has given me St Thérèse, Rachel and Sister Wendy and through them I have learnt that God is all compassionate, all loving. The Catholic Church has also given me great confidence that everyone, no matter what anyone else thinks of them, is very precious and special, and whatever wrong anyone might have done, there is always a reason. Perhaps they are scarred in some way, and God understands that. No human being can really judge another person's actions. I wouldn't feel cut off from God, no matter what I did. Anything can be forgiven if a person is truly sorry.

In spite of my criticisms of the Church I have never considered joining another Church because I still love it and am totally happy in the Catholic Church. I also love other Churches and I'm not saying the Catholic Church is the only Church that is totally right, but it's right for me.

I wrote a book about prayer, *Journey to God,* and the first line was 'Prayer is something God does'. I do not think I have got all the answers, but what I am trying to say is that the important thing is to give space and time and what happens in that is really God's work. The great thing I learnt from reading St Thérèse was that true prayer means letting go, letting God take over. She was in her convent for fifteen years and, during the daily silent prayer, for nine of those years she fell asleep every time. That says everything about it. It's what happens in that secret part of you; you just have to get in touch with your own spirituality.